the narrative path

D1026324

the narrative path

the later works of paul ricoeur

edited by
t. peter kemp and david rasmussen

The MIT Press
Cambridge, Massachusetts
London, England

First MIT Press edition, 1989

This work originally appeared as volume 14, no. 2, of the journal
Philosophy and Social Criticism

© 1988 *Philosophy and Social Criticism*

Printed and bound in the United States of America.

Library of Congress Cataloging-in-Publication Data

The Narrative path : the later works of Paul Ricoeur / (edited by) T.
    Peter Kemp and David Rasmussen.
        p.   cm.
    ISBN 0-262-11147-0. — ISBN 0-262-61060-4 (pbk.)
    1. Ricoeur, Paul—Contributions hermeneutics. 2. Hermeneutics.
3. Narration (Rhetoric) 4. Metaphor. 5. Ricoeur, Paul-
-Bibliography. I. Kemp, T. Peter. II. Rasmussen, David M.
B2430.R554N37 1989
194—dc20   89-35975
                                             CIP

table of contents

introduction

This anthology on Paul Ricoeur's philosophy focuses on the latest development of his ideas, especially as presented in his great work, **Time and Narrative**, published by Chicago University Press in three volumes (1984-1988).

Richard Kearney and Maria Villela Petit do not limit themselves to dealing with Ricoeur's latest publications, however, as they extend the perspective backwards to clarify some recurrent themes in his philosophy; Kearney concentrates on the role of imagination for hermeneutics, and Petit on how Ricoeur's historical reflections develop from **History and Truth** to **Time and Narrative**.

Two others extend the significance of his reflection on metaphoric and narrative language respectively to poetry and ethics. Serge Meitinger analyzes the relation between time and poetry from the point of view of Ricoeur's reflection on the connection between time and narrative, and T. Peter Kemp shows that narration is indispensable to ethics if one follows Ricoeur's claim that narratives are prefigured in the world of action and aim its refiguration.

Finally, space is given to Paul Ricoeur himself, who reveals his view of the human subject at different levels: linguistic, practical introduction and ethical. Here, once again, Ricoeur demonstrates his famous ability for synthesizing not only analytical and phenomenological philosophies, but also the different aspects of the human being as subject-matter of philosophical reflection.

Additionally, thanks to Frans Vansina, we are able to present an up-to-date selected bibliography of Ricoeur's works in English.

The papers of Maria Villela Petit, Serge Meitinger and T. Peter Kemp were presented in French at the Ricoeur Conference at Cerisy-la-Salle, France, August 1988.

T. Peter Kemp
David M. Rasmussen

richard kearney
paul ricoeur and the hermeneutic imagination

Most phenomenological accounts of imagination have concentrated on its role as **vision**, as a special or modified way of **seeing** the world. Imagination is thus defined in terms of its relation to perception, be it positive or negative, continuous or discontinuous. Husserl describes the act of imagining as a "neutralized" mode of seeing, Sartre as an "unrealized" mode of quasi-seeing, and Merleau-Ponty as a dialectical complement of seeing.

This privileging of the visual model is no doubt related to the primary role granted to "description" in the phenomenological method. With the hermeneutic turn in phenomenology, this privilege is significantly revised. As one moves from description to interpretation, from *Wesenschau* to *Verstehen*, the imagination is considered less in terms of "vision" than in terms of "language." Or to put it more exactly, imagination is assessed as an indispensable agent in the creation of meaning in and through language—what Ricoeur calls "semantic innovation."

Paul Ricoeur provides us with the most impressive example of such a hermeneutics of imagination.[1] While his early works—**Freedom and Nature** (1950) in particular—conformed to the descriptive conventions of eidetic phenomenology, the publication of **The Symbolism of Evil** in 1960 introduced a "hermeneutic" model of analysis which opened up the possibility of a new appreciation of the linguistic functioning of imagination. This was to be the first of a number of works in which Ricoeur would explore the creative role of imagination in language—be it in the guise of symbols, myths, poems, narratives or ideologies. The following study proposes to isolate some of the key steps in Ricoeur's hermeneutic exploration of imagination—an exploration which, it should be noted at the outset, is less systematic than episodic in nature. Ricoeur's tentative and always provisional probing of a poetic hermeneutic of imagination represents, I believe, the ultimate, if discreet, agenda of his philosophical project. That, at least, is the hypothesis that guides my reading of his work below—my own hermeneutic wager regarding his hermeneutic wager.

The Linguistic Imagination

Insofar as hermeneutics is concerned with double or multiple levels of meaning, it is evident that images can no longer be adequately understood in terms of their immediate phenomenological **appearance** to consciousness. Replacing the visual model of the image with the verbal, Ricoeur affirms the more **poetical** role of imagining—that is, its ability to say one thing in terms of another, or to say several things at the same time, thereby creating something **new**. The crucial role played by imagination in this process of "semantic innovation" was to become one of the abiding concerns of the later philosophy of Ricoeur.

The problem of semantic innovation remained unresolved for Sartre, for example, who in **L'Imaginaire**, argued that imagination was condemned to an "essential poverty." The imaginary could not teach us anything new since it was held to be a "nothingness" projected by our consciousness. The cognitive content of an image presupposed, accordingly, our prior contact with the perceptual world (from which all our knowledge arises). The imaginary world, for Sartre, is a **negation** of the perceptual world. It is not a simultaneous juxtaposing of two different worlds which produces a new meaning, as Ricoeur would argue.

Before proceeding to a more detailed account of Ricoeur's own original contribution to the philosophy of imagination, it may be useful to first cite Ricoeur's critical summary of the available theories of images and imagining. In an essay entitled, "L'Imagination dans le discours et dans l'action" in **Du Texte à l'action** (1986), Ricoeur adverts to the problematic and often confused nature of modern philosophies of the image. He argues that the radical equivocity at the very heart of the imaginative activity has led to a series of rival, and often mutually exclusive,

ricoeur and hermeneutic imagination

accounts. These accounts are located by Ricoeur in terms of two opposite axes. On the one hand they explain the process of imagining in terms of the **object**: a typical example of this being Hume's empiricist account of the image as a faded trace of perception, a weakened impression preserved and re-presented in memory. Toward this pole of the image gravitate the theories of the **reproductive** imagination. On the other hand, we find theories which explain our imaginative activity in terms of the **subject**, that is, in terms of a human consciousness that is fascinated or freed by its own images. An example of this latter theory would be the German idealist and romantic accounts of the **productive** imagination from Kant and Schelling to the existentialist descriptions of Sartre in **L'Imaginaire**. But this basic distinction between the reproductive and productive roles of imagination does not resolve the aporetic nature of our inherited understanding of imagining. Ricoeur extends the problematic horizons of this debate as follows:

The productive imagination, and even the reproductive to the extent that it comprises the minimal initiative concerning the evocation of something absent, operates ... according to whether the subject of imagination is capable or not of assuming a critical consciousness of the difference between the real and the imaginary. The theories of the image here divide up along an axis which is no longer noematic but noetic, and whose variations are regulated by degrees of belief. At one end of the axis, that of a non-critical consciousness, the image is confused with the real, mistaken for the real. This is the power of the lie or error denounced by Pascal; and it is also, **mutatis mutandis**, *the* **imaginatio** *of Spinoza, contaminated by belief for as long as a contrary belief has not dislodged it from its primary position. At the other end of the axis, where the critical distance is fully conscious of itself, imagination is the very instrument of the critique of reality. The transcendental reduction of Husserl, as a neutralization of existence, is the most complete instance of this. The variations of meaning along this second axis are no less ample than the above. What after all could be in common between the* **state of confusion** *which characterizes that consciousness which unknown to itself takes for real what for another consciousness is not real, and the* **act of distinction** *which, highly self-conscious, enables consciousness to posit something at a distance from the real and thus produce the alterity at the very heart of existence?*

Such is the knot of aporias which is revealed by an overview of the ruins which today constitute the theory of imagination. Do these aporias themselves betray a fault in the philosophy of imagination or the structural feature of imagination itself which it would be the task of philosophy to take account of?[2]

3

Ricoeur appears to answer yes to both sides of the question. The "fault," in other words, of most philosophies of imagination to date has been their failure to develop a properly hermeneutic account of imagining as an inherently symbolizing-metaphorizing-narrativizing activity—that is, its most basic "structural feature" of semantic innovation.

The adoption of hermeneutics—as the "art of deciphering indirect meanings"—acknowledges the **symbolizing** power of imagination. This power, to transform given meanings into new ones, enables one to construe the future as the "possible theatre of my liberty," as an horizon of hope. The existential implications of this approach are crucial. The age-old antagonism between will and necessity (or in Sartre's terms, between *l'imaginaire* as *pour-soi* and *le réel* as *en-soi*) is now seen to be surmountable. "We have thought too much," observes Ricoeur, "in terms of a will which submits and not enough in terms of an imagination which opens up."[3]

Ricoeur's preference for a semantic model of imagination over a visual one makes possible a new appreciation of this properly creative role of imagination. If images are **spoken** before they are **seen**, as Ricoeur maintains, they can no longer be construed as quasi-material residues of perception (as empiricism believed), nor indeed as modifications or negations of perception (as eidetic phenomenology tended to believe). Ricoeur's privileging of the "poetical" functioning of images illustrates his conviction that the productive power of imagination is primarily verbal. The example of a verbal metaphor in poetry epitomizes the way in which imagination conjoins two semantic fields, making what is predicatively impertinent at a literal level into something predicatively pertinent at a new (poetic) level. Or to use Ricoeur's graphic phrase: "Imagination comes into play in that moment when a new meaning emerges from out of the ruins of the literal interpretation."[4]

Taking up Aristotle's definition of a good metaphor in the **Poetics** (1459a, 4-8) as the apprehension of **similarity**, Ricoeur points out that what is meant here is not similarity between already similar ideas (for such a role would be redundant) but similarity between semantic fields hitherto considered **dissimilar**. It is the "semantic shock" engendered by the coming together of two different meanings which produces a **new** meaning. And imagination, Ricoeur claims, is precisely this power of metaphorically reconciling opposing meanings, forging an unprecedented semantic pertinence from an old semantic impertinence. So that if one wants to say with Wittgenstein, for example, that imagining is a "seeing-as" (seeing one thing in terms of another) this is only the case insofar as the linguistic

ricoeur and hermeneutic imagination

power of conjoining different semantic fields is already at work—at least implicitly.

This is a decisive point in Ricoeur's argument. It emphasizes that what matters in imagination is less the **content** than the **function** of images. This specific function is understood here both in terms of an intentional projection of possible meanings (the phenomenological-hermeneutic model) and a schematizing synthesis of the many under the guise of the same (the Kantian model). It is this twin function of projection and schematism which accounts for imagination as "the operation of grasping the similar in a predicative assimilation responding to a semantic clash between dissimilar meanings."[5] Ricoeur thus links the productive power of language and that of imagination. For new meanings to come into being they need to be spoken or uttered in the form of new verbal images. And this requires that the phenomenological account of imagining as **appearance** be supplemented by its hermeneutic account as **meaning**. Imagination can be recognized accordingly as the act of responding to a demand for new meaning, the demand of emerging realities to **be** by **being said** in new ways. And it is for this reason that Ricoeur frequently invokes Bachelard's famous phrase that "a poetic image, by its novelty, sets in motion the entire linguistic mechanism. The poetic image places us at the origin of the speaking being."[6]

A poetic imagination is one which creates meaning by responding to the desire of being to be expressed. It is a Janus facing in two directions at once—back to the being that is being revealed and forward to the language that is revealing. And at the level of language itself, it also does double-duty, for it produces a text which opens up new horizons of meaning for the reader. The poetic imagination liberates the reader into a free space of possibility, suspending the reference to the immediate world of perception (both the author's and the reader's) and thereby disclosing "new ways of being in the world."[7] The function of "semantic innovation"—which is most proper to imagination—is therefore, in its most fundamental sense, an **ontological** event. The innovative power of linguistic imagination is not some "decorative excess or effusion of subjectivity, but the capacity of language to open up new worlds."[8] The function of imagination in poetry or myth, for example, is defined accordingly as the "disclosure of unprecedented worlds, an opening onto possible worlds which transcend the limits of our actual world."[9]

To account for this phenomenon of ontological novelty, Ricoeur's hermeneutics of imagination looks beyond the first-order reference to empirical reality—which ordinary language discourse normally lays claim to—to a second-order reference to an horizon of possible worlds. A hermeneutic approach to

5

imagination thus differs from a structuralist or existentialist one in its concentration on "the capacity of world-disclosure yielded by texts." In short, hermeneutics is not confined to the **objective** structural analysis of texts, nor to the **subjective** existential analysis of the authors of texts; its primary concern is with the **worlds** which these authors and texts open up.[10]

An understanding of the possible worlds opened up by the poetic imagination also permits a new understanding of ourselves as beings-in-the-world. But, for Ricoeur, the hermeneutic circle precludes any short cut to immediate self-understanding. The human subject can only come to know itself through the hermeneutic detour of interpreting signs—that is, by deciphering the meanings contained in myths, symbols and dreams produced by the human imagination. The shortest route from the self to itself is through the images of others.

The hermeneutic imagination is not confined, however, to circles of **interpretation**. By projecting new worlds it also provides us with projects of **action**. In fact the traditional opposition between *theoria* and *praxis* dissolves to the extent that "imagination has a projective function which pertains to the very dynamism of action."[11] The metaphors, symbols or narratives produced by imagination all provide us with "imaginative variations" of the world, thereby offering us the freedom to conceive of the world in new ways and to undertake forms of action which might lead to its transformation. Semantic innovation can thus point towards social transformation. The possible worlds of imagination can be made real by action. And this is surely what Ricoeur has in mind when he says that there can be "no action without imagination." We shall return to this crucial aspect of Ricoeur's argument in our discussion of the "social imagination" below.

The Symbolic Imagination

Having offered a summary outline of some of the key features of Ricoeur's hermeneutic account of imagination, I now propose to take a more systematic approach by examining the following four categories, which broadly correspond to consecutive phases in the later (that is, hermeneutic) philosophy of Paul Ricoeur: 1) **The Symbolic Imagination**; 2) **The Oneiric Imagination**; 3) **The Poetic Imagination**; and 4) **The Social Imagination**.

The publication of **Le Symbolique du Mal** in 1960 marked Ricoeur's transition from a phenomenology of will to a hermeneutics of symbol. It signalled a departure from descriptive phenomenology, as a reflection on intentional modes of consciousness, in favor of a larger hermeneutic conviction, i.e., that meaning is never simply the intuitive possession of a subject but is always mediated through signs and symbols of our intersubjective existence. Henceforth, an understanding of consciousness would involve an interpretation of culture.

In **The Symbolism of Evil**, Ricoeur shows that a rigorous interpretation of the founding myths of western culture (e.g., Adam, Prometheus, Oedipus) enables us to disclose the symbolic relation of the human subject to meaning. Suspending the conventional definition of myth as a "false **explanation** by means of fables," Ricoeur attempts to recover myth's genuinely **exploratory** function. Once we accept that myth cannot and does not provide us with a scientific account of the way things really are, we can begin to properly appreciate its legitimate creative role as a **symbolizing** power.

What is a symbol for Ricoeur? A symbol is a double intentionality, wherein one meaning is transgressed or transcended by another. As such, it is a work of imagination which enables being to emerge as language (signification) and, by extension, as thought (interpretation). Whence Ricoeur's famous hermeneutic maxim *"Le symbole donne à penser."* There are three principle categories of symbol examined by Ricoeur: **cosmic**, **oneiric** and **poetic**.

(a) Cosmic symbols refer to a human's primary act of reading the sacred **on** the world. Here the human imagination interprets aspects of the world—the heavens, the sun, the moon, the waters—**as** signs of some ultimate meaning. At this most basic level, the symbol is both a thing and a sign: it embodies and signifies the sacred at one and the same time.[12] Or to put it in another way, when dealing with cosmic symbols, the imagination reads the things of the world as signs and signs as things of the world. As such, the symbolic imagination is already, at least implicitly, **linguistic**. Ricoeur makes this clear in the following passage from **Freud and Philosophy**: "These symbols are not inscribed **beside** language, as modes of immediate expression, directly perceptible visages; it is in the universe of discourse that these realities take on a symbolic dimension. Even when it is the elements of the world that carry the symbol—earth, sky, water, life—it is the word (of consecration, invocation or mythic narrative) which **says** their cosmic expressivity thanks to the double meaning of the **words** earth, sky, water, life" (that is, their obvious literal meaning as references to things and their ulterior meaning, e.g., water as a symbol of renewed spiritual life). Ricoeur can thus affirm that the "expressivity of the world comes to language through the symbol as double meaning."[13] For a cosmic symbol—like any other kind—occurs whenever "language produces composite signs where the meaning, not content to designate something directly, points to another meaning which can only be reached (indirectly) by means of this designation."[14] Illustrating this linguistic property of symbols, Ricoeur comments on the phrase from the Psalms: "The skies tell of the glory of God" as follows: "The skies don't speak themselves; rather, they are spoken by the prophet, by the hymn, by the liturgy. One always needs the word to assume the world into a manifestation of the sacred (hierophany)."[15] And here he cites the view of the structural anthropologist, Dumézil, that "it is under the sign of the *logos* and not under that of *mana* that research in the history of religions takes its stand today" (Preface to M. Eliade, **Traité d'Histoire des Religions**).

(b) In the second category of symbols—the oneiric or dream image—we witness a shift from the cosmic to the psychic function of imagination. Here Ricoeur talks of complementing a phenomenology of religious symbols (à la Eliade) with a psychoanalysis of unconscious symbols. To this end, he invokes the works of Freud and Jung who investigated links between the symbols of the individual unconscious and symbols as "common representations of the culture or folklore of humanity as a whole."[16] Ricoeur spells out the rapport between cosmic and oneiric symbols as follows: "To manifest the 'sacred' **on** the 'cosmos' and to manifest it **in** the 'psyche' are the same thing... Cosmos and psyche are two poles of the same 'expressivity': I express myself in expressing the world."[17] It is precisely this expressive function of the psychic or oneiric image which establishes its intimate relation to language. As Ricoeur remarks, dream images must be "originally close to words since they can be told, communicated."[18]

(c) The third modality of symbols—the "poetic imagination"—completes the double "expressivity" of cosmos and psyche. It is here that the creative powers of imagination are most evident and receive explicit acknowledgement from Ricoeur. In fact, it is only in this third category that Ricoeur (in **The Symbolism of Evil**) uses the term "imagination" in any systematic sense. It is the poetical perspective, he argues, which enables us to draw back from both the religious images of cosmology and the dream images of psychoanalysis, disclosing the symbolic function of the image per se in its nascent state. In poetry, Ricoeur maintains, the symbol reveals the welling up of language—"language in a state of emergence"—instead of regarding it in its hieratic stability under the protection of rites and myths, as in the history of religion, or instead of deciphering it through the resurgences of a suppressed infancy.[19] In this sense, the poetical is the epitome of the symbolic imagination.

Ricoeur insists, however, that these three levels of symbolism are not unconnected. The structure of poetic imagination is also that of the dream as it draws from the fragments of our past a projection of our future; and it is also that, at bottom, of hierophanies which disclose the heavens and the earth as images of the sacred. In all three instances what is at issue is not the image-as-representation but the image-as-sign. Ricoeur returns to this crucial distinction again and again. In **The Symbolism of Evil** he does so in terms of a differentiation between the static model of the image as "portrait" and the dynamic model of the image as "expression." In **Freud and Philosophy**, he uses the opposition **image-representation** and **image-verb**. But whatever the particular formulation, what Ricoeur is concerned with is a critique of the representational model of the image as a mere negation of perceptual reality. And this critique is not only levelled at the standard empiricist account of Hume, but also at the phenomenological account of Sartre. The following passage from the introduction to **The Symbolism of Evil** makes this clear: "It is necessary firmly to distinguish imagination from image, if by image is understood a function of absence, the annulment of the real in an imaginary unreal. This image-representation, conceived on the model of a portrait of the absent, is still too dependent on the thing that it makes unreal; it remains a process for **making present** to oneself the things of the world. A poetic image is much closer to a word than to a portrait."[20] To be fair to Sartre, however, one would have to recall that while most of his examples of the "unrealizing" function of imaging are drawn from visual representation (picturing Pierre in Berlin, the portrait of King Charles, etc.), he does go to pains to establish the image as a dynamic act of consciousness rather than a quasi-perceptual thing in consciousness. But that said, it is true that he, and Husserl before him, fails to adequately grasp the fact that signification and imagination are not two separate *sui generis* modes of intentionality but are inextricably related. It is for this reason that Ricoeur clearly prefers the position of Bachelard, which he approvingly cites: "The poetic image becomes a new being of our language, it expresses us in making us that which it expresses."[21]

The essential point to retain from Ricoeur's hermeneutic analysis of the three kinds of symbol—cosmic, oneiric and poetic—is that they all find expression in and through a **linguistic** imagination. This is stated most succinctly in **Freud and Philosophy** when Ricoeur affirms that "it is always in language that the cosmos, that desire, and that the imaginary, come into words."[22]

There is no doubt that **The Symbolism of Evil** concentrates on the first category of symbol—the cosmic. This first phase of the hermeneutic project is described by Ricoeur as a "re-enactment in sympathetic imagination" of the foundational myths where Western [wo]man sought to communicate his or her first experiences of the cosmos. (Myths are understood as symbolic stories—or to be more precise, as "species of symbols developed in the form of narration and articulated in a time and a space that cannot be co-ordinated with the time and space of history and geography."[23]) This hermeneutic act of sympathetically re-imagining the cosmic images of our foundational myths demands that Ricoeur abandon the original phenomenological dream of a "philosophy without presuppositions." Indeed, it presupposes that which descriptive phenomenology often tended to ignore—language. The hermeneutics of symbols must begin from a full language, that is, from the recognition that before reflection and intuition **there are already symbols**. "It is by beginning with a symbolism already there," as Ricoeur notes, "that we give ourselves something to think about."[24]

This hermeneutic task of recovering language in its symbolic fullness is, for Ricoeur, a singularly modern one. It is precisely because language has become so formalized, transparent and technical in the contempoary era that the need is all the greater to rediscover language's creative powers of symbolization. This is not a matter of nostalgia for a lost Atlantis. It is a task animated by the "hope for a re-creation of language."[25] And it also involves a critical project. For it is only by demythologizing the abuses of myth (e.g. as a false explanation of reality) that we can demythologize our contemporary language—that is, restore to it the poetic and symbolic powers of imagination. "The dissolution of the myth as (false) explanation is the necessary way to the restoration of the myth as symbolism," writes Ricoeur. If demythologization is the possible gain of a modern attention to objective truth, this should not prevent the modern hermeneutic task of reunifying the various fields of meaning by renewing "contact with the fundamental symbols of consciousness."[26] In short, we need to combine the critical gesture of modernity with the symbolizing gesture of myth if we are to develop an adequate hermeneutic of the human imagination. Instead of adopting the reductive approach of an "allegorical" reading—which would seek to uncover a disguised message beneath the image-symbols of a myth—Ricoeur advances a hermeneutic imagination which would, on the contrary, "start from the symbols and endeavor to promote the meaning, to form it, by means of creative interpretation."[27] This is, I suspect, what Ricoeur has in mind when he suggests that it is by "interpreting that we can hear again."

The Oneiric Imagination

Whereas Ricoeur had concerned himself in **The Symbolism of Evil** with one particular field of symbols—those related primarily to mythic accounts of evil—in **Freud and Philosophy** he enlarges the inquiry to analyse the "epistemology of the symbol" as it manifests itself in the desires of the unconscious.[28] The dream image shows, in exemplary fashion, how we can say things other than what we are ostensibly saying; how behind direct meanings there are indirect ones. Because of this double intentionality, symbols are what make "poets of every dreamer."[29]

The poet is the dreamer writ large. And what is important here is the suggestion that symbols are essentially "image-words" which traverse and transcend "image-representations." Imagination is not simply a "power of images" to represent absent objects. The visual images of dreams are sensory vehicles for verbal images which transcend them and designate **other** meanings than the literal ones. Thus psychoanalysis recognized that dream images call forth narrative interpretation. It is precisely because dreams—like myths and poems—operate according to a depth language of double meanings that they can be recounted and deciphered. Dreams want to tell themselves. They give rise to speech, to thought, to narration. The dreamer feels closed off in a private world until the dream is recounted. And this power of recounting is exemplified, for Ricoeur, in the poetic imagination which exposes the "birth of the word such as it was buried within the enigmas of...the psyche."[30]

But if poetry represents the positive pole of dreams, dissimulation represents its negative pole. The basic hermeneutic lesson to be gleaned from dreams, according to Ricoeur, is that images can serve to **mask** as well as to disclose meanings. The work of dream images provides ample evidence of the fact that the symbolic levels of sense are far more complex and oblique than the traditional models of analogy and allegory would allow. Along with Marx and Nietzsche, Freud was to champion a modern **hermeneutics of suspicion,** alert to the distorting and falsifying potential of images. Each of these three "masters of suspicion," as Ricoeur calls them, approached images as devices for concealing hidden motivations. For Nietzsche this was the will to power, for Marx class struggle, and for Freud the neurotic repression of desire. The latter developed the method of psychoanalysis, accordingly, as a means of detecting the censoring function of dream images—the primary function of this method being to "disclose the variety of elaborate procedures which interpose between apparent and latent meanings."[31]

Psychoanalysis calls for the hermeneutic function of critical interpretation by showing how images are not innocent, how they conceal as well as reveal meaning, how they deform as well as disclose intentions. It is the double texture of dream images—the internal transgression of one meaning by another—that invites, even provokes, our critical interpretation. Or as Ricoeur puts it,

richard kearney

"every *mythos* carries a latent *logos* which demands to be exposed—where someone dreams...another rises up to interpret."[32]

But if psychoanalysis promotes a hermeneutics of **suspicion**, it also points toward a hermeneutics of **affirmation**. While the former examines how images disguise hidden meanings drawn from our private or collective past, by means of an "archaeological" reference back to an experience which precedes them, the latter shows how dream-images can open up new dimensions of meaning by virtue of a "teleological" reference to new worlds of possibility. Because desire is the basic motivation of all such dream-images, as Freud argued, these images are ways of **saying** this desire. And they do this either by dissimulating it in other guises or by expressing a passion for possibilities not yet realized. Insofar as this second option is concerned, the desire of dream-images invents a future and thus aspires to a condition of creation, *poiesis*, poetry. It generates a surplus of meaning (*surcroît du sens*).[33] And this surplus is proof of a level of meaning which is irreducible to a retrospective correspondence between the image of one's dream and a literal event of one's past experience. Or as Bachelard put it, "you cannot explain the flower by the fertilizer." It is this productive power of images—which Freud recognized in the *eros* of dreams—which ensures that any adequate hermeneutic of imagination must extend beyond an "archaeology of the unconscious" to include both a "teleology of desire" and an "eschatology of the sacred."

In **The Conflict of Interpretations** (1969), Ricoeur elaborates on this dual function of the hermeneutic imagination—as **recollection** and **projection**. He writes: "We may fully comprehend the hermeneutic problem if we are able to grasp the double dependence of the self on the (symbolic images of) the **unconscious** and the **sacred**—since this dependence is only made manifest through the modality of symbolism. In order to illustrate this double dependency, reflection must humble consciousness and interpret it through symbolic significations, rising up from **behind** or in **front** of consciousness, **beneath** or **beyond** it. In short, reflection must include an archaeology and an eschatology."[34]

Ricoeur argues, moreover, that prophecy needs demystification. By unmasking the falsifying function of certain dream-images, with the help of a psychoanalytic model of "suspicion," we may find ourselves in a better position to subsequently restore aspects of these images as "signs of the sacred." Without the hermeneutic detour of suspicion we would not be in a position to discriminate between those images which are merely a "return to the repressed" (in Freud's phrase) and those which serve as symbols of an eschatological horizon of possibility. Indeed, it is less a matter of discriminating between regressive images on the one hand and progressive images on the other. Every utopian image contains an archaic element and vice versa. Images of the mythic past are often used to allude prophetically to an *eschaton* still to come. And the eschatology of imagination is always, as Ricoeur puts it, a creative repetition of its archaeology. "The progressive order of symbols is not external to the regressive order of phantasms. In plunging into the archaic mythologies of the unconscious new signs of the sacred rise up."[35]

A critical hermeneutic of imagination, as Ricoeur learns from Freud, is one which demystifies the dissimulating property of phantasms in order to release the symbolizing power of images. Idols must be unmasked so that symbols may speak. And an additional reminder which hermeneutics receives from psychoanalysis is that the images of the unconscious are charged with multiple meanings which are irreducible to the level of a one to one rational correspondence. They provoke rational interpretation; but the rational interpretation can never exhaust them. For even when infantile or archaic images are deciphered in terms of their regressive reference to the past, there always remains a **surplus** which points towards an inexhaustible creativity of meaning. This is where Ricoeur locates his wager that new meanings **can** emerge, that things as they are **can** change. "Liberty according to hope," he writes in **The Conflict of Interpretations**, "is nothing other when understood psychologically, than this creative imagining of the possible."[36]

It is this double axis of archaeological and eschatological reference which signals the failure of all theories which seek to reduce the oneiric imagination to a system of speculative reason. It reminds us that there is always more to imagination than has ever been dreamt of in our philosophies. Moreover, it is due to this **excess** of imagination over reason that symbols call forth a multiplicity of meanings which in turn give rise to a multiplicity of readings—psychoanalytic (Freud), religious (Eliade), philosophical (Hegel), etc. This is why a hermeneutic of imagination culminates not in absolute knowledge but in an endless conflict of interpretations.

The Poetical Imagination

Having concentrated on a hermeneutics of mythic and oneiric symbols in his three major works of the sixties—**The Symbolism of Evil, Freud and Philosophy** and **The Conflict of Interpretations**—Ricoeur devoted most of his attention in the seventies and eighties to a detailed investigation of the "poetical"

richard
kearney

expressions of imagination. This more recent phase of Ricoeur's hermeneutic project includes **The Rule of Metaphor** (1975) as well as his three volume **Time and Narrative** (1984-85). Ricoeur comments on this new phase in his work as follows: "In **The Rule of Metaphor** I try to show how language could extend itself to its very limits forever discovering new resonances within itself. The term *vive* in the French title *la Métaphore Vive* is all important, for it was my purpose to demonstrate that there is not just an epistemological and political imagination, but also, and perhaps more fundamentally, a **linguistic imagination** which generates and regenerates meaning through the living powers of metaphoricity." And of his three volume study of narrative he adds: "**Time and Narrative** develops this inquiry into the inventive power of language. Here the analysis of narrative operations in a literary text, for instance, can teach us how we formulate a new structure of 'time' by creating new modes of plot and characterization...how narrativity, as the construction or deconstruction of paradigms of story-telling, is a perpetual search for new ways of expressing human time, a production or creation of meaning."[37]

In **The Rule of Metaphor**, as in other works, Ricoeur deals with imagination in a fragmentary rather than systematic fashion. It is, as it were, a hidden prompter guiding and motivating his delivery without ever occupying center stage in the process of explication. Describing the innovative power of metaphorical imagination in terms of the ability to establish similarity in dissimilarity, Ricoeur points out that he has now progressed from an analysis of the creative tension between meanings in words (symbols) to that between meanings in sentences (metaphors). Or to put it in another way, in metaphor the productive unit is no longer the **word** but the **sentence**. It is at the level of the sentence that metaphor expresses the power of imagination to create a new semantic unit out of two different ideas. "It is in the moment of the emergence of a new meaning from the ruins of literal predication that imagination offers its specific mediation."[38] It is in this context that Ricoeur offers one of his most explicit formulations of the distinction between verbal and non-verbal imagination. Borrowing Kant's terminology he identifies the former with the productive imagination and the latter with the reproductive. "Would not imagination have something to do with the conflict between identity and difference?" he asks. And he makes it clear that he is not speaking here of "imagination in its sensible, quasi-sensual aspect"—in other words, the **non-verbal** kernal of imagination.

On the contrary, he argues that the "only way to approach the problem of imagination from the perspective of a semantic theory, that is to say on a verbal plane, is to begin with productive imagination in the Kantian sense, and to put off reproductive imagination or imagery as long as possible. Treated as a schema, the image presents a verbal dimension; before being the gathering-point of faded perceptions, it is that of emerging meanings." Placing himself thus in the camp of Kant rather than of Hume, Ricoeur goes on to explain that the metaphor works in the same way as the schema insofar as it functions as "the matrix of a new semantic pertinence that is born out of the dismantling of semantic networks caused by the shock of contradiction." The metaphoric function of imagination thus involves a verbal aspect to the extent that it involves "grasping identity within differences," establishing the "relatedness of terms far apart" in such a way that they confront each other rather than fuse together. This schematism of metaphor, affirms Ricoeur, "turns imagination into the place where the figurative meaning emerges in the interplay of identity and difference."[39]

And yet the imagination needs images. Without any visual aspect, the verbal imagination would remain an invisible productivity. So what remains to be demonstrated is the sensible moment of metaphoric imagination. And this is where Ricoeur calls for a [phenomenological] psychology of **seeing-as** to complement a semantics of creative **saying**. For if the productive imagination were confined to a purely verbal innovation it would cease to be **imagination**. Ricoeur seeks accordingly to anchor a psychology of the imaginary in a semantic theory of metaphor. "Seeing-as" provides a key as the sensible aspect of poetic imagination. It holds sense and image together in an intuitive manner. It selects from the quasi-sensory mass of imagery producing a certain semantic order. And it can also work contrariwise to bring conceptual meaning to intuitive fullness, as in the example of reading: "The **seeing as** activated in reading ensures the joining of verbal meaning with imagistic fullness. And this conjunction is no longer something outside language since it can be reflected as a relationship. **Seeing as** contains a ground, a foundation, this is precisely, resemblance." Ricoeur can thus conclude that "seeing as" plays the role of a schema which unites the **empty** concept and the **blind** impression: "[T]hanks to its character as half thought and half experience, it joins the light of sense with the fullness of the image. In this way, the non-verbal and the verbal are firmly united at the core of the image-ing function of language."[40]

But the metaphorical imagination not only combines the verbal and the non-verbal, it also produces new meaning by confronting a literal with a figurative sense. This **tensional** theory of metaphor is most obvious in the case of a living metaphor such as Hopkins, "Oh! The mind has mountains" where a literal **is not** (the reader knows that literally the mind does not have mountains) is accompanied by a metaphorical **is**. This power to transform contradiction into new meaning is evident in the metaphorical function of "seeing *x* as *y*"—for while we know *x* **is not** *y*, at a literal level, we affirm that it **is** it, at an imaginative level. Metaphor is living by virtue of the fact that it introduces the spark of imagination into a "thinking more" (*penser plus*).[41] And this "thinking more"— which is at root a saying-seeing more—attests to the curious paradox that the "concept of imagination, in the context of a theory of metaphor centered around the notion of semantic innovation" is also a "logic of *discovery*."[42]

Having brought his semantic theory of imagination to its limits— to the frontier point of exchange between **saying** and **seeing as**—Ricoeur invokes once again Bachelard's phenomenology of imagination as an avenue to explore the ontological depths of this interaction between verbal and non-verbal imagination: "Bachelard has taught us that the image is not a residue of impression, but an aura surrounding speech...The poem gives birth to the image; the poetic image "is at once a becoming of expression and a becoming of our being. Here expression creates being...one could not meditate in a zone that preceded language."[43] The poetic image thus points to the very "depths of existence" where "a new being in language" is synonymous with a "growth in being" itself. It is because there is poetical imagination that words dream being.

The hermeneutic analysis of the role played by imagination in the metaphorical play of language leads Ricoeur to the crucial ontological paradox of **creation-as-discovery**. "Through the recovery of the capacity of language to create and recreate, we **discover** reality itself in the process of being **created**... Language in the making celebrates reality in the making."[44] Ricoeur can thus conclude that the strategy of discourse implied in metaphorical languages is...to shatter and to increase our sense of reality by shattering and increasing our language...with metaphor we experience the metamorphosis of both language and reality."[45] At this point in his reflections on metaphor, Ricoeur approximates to the Aristotle of the **Poetics**, for whom it was vain to ask whether "the universal that poetry 'teaches', already existed **before** it was **invented**. It is as much found as invented."[46]

In **Time and Narrative**, Ricoeur develops some of these ontological implications of "metaphorical" reference. He shows how poetical language—be it lyrical or narrative—reveals a capacity for non-descriptive reference which exceeds the immediate reference of our everyday language. While poetical reference suspends literal reference and thereby appears to make language refer only to itself (as the structuralists argued), it in fact reveals a deeper and more radical power of reference to those ontological aspects of our being-in-the-world that cannot be spoken of **directly**. **Seeing as** thus not only implies a **saying as** but also a **being as**. Ricoeur relates this power of poetic imagination to creatively redescribe and reinvent being to the narrative power of "emplotment" (*mise-en-intrigue*). Borrowing François Dagognet's term **iconic augmentation**, he makes the point that the role of the image or *Bild* is to bring about an increase in the being of our vision of the world which is impoverished by everyday affairs. "We owe a large part of the enlarging of our horizon of existence to poetic works. Far from producing only weakened images of reality—shadows, as in the Platonic treatment of the *eikon* in painting or writing (**Phædrus** 274e-77e)—literary works depict reality by **augmenting** it with meanings that themselves depend upon the virtues of abbreviation, saturation and culmination, so strikingly illustrated by emplotment."[47]

Ricoeur here rejoins the ontological hermeneutics of Heidegger and Gadamer that, in contradistinction to romantic hermeneutics, aims less at restoring the author's intention behind the text than at making explicit the movement by which the text unfolds, as it were, a world in front of itself.[48] The poetical imagination at work in a text is one which augments my power of being-in-the-world: "what is interpreted in a text is the proposing of a world that I might inhabit and into which I might project my ownmost powers."[49] Ricoeur thus places the referential capacity of narrative works under those of poetic works in general. For if the poetic metaphor redescribes the world, "in the same way...making a narratif resignifies the world in its temporal dimension, to the extent that narrating, telling, reciting is to remake action following the poem's invention."[50]

Every **historical narrative** borrows from this imaginative power of redescription since insofar as it constitutes a "reference through traces" "the past can only be reconstructed by the imagination."[51] But it is clearly in **fictional narrative** that the productive power of human imagination to configure and refigure human time is most dramatically evident. Presupposed by both historical and fictional narrative, however, is the pre-narrative capacity of human imagination to exist and to act in the world in a symbolically significant manner. For human being-in-the-world, in its most everyday sense—as Kant and Heidegger realized— involves a process of **temporalization** which makes our present actions meaningful by interpreting them in terms of a recollected past and a projected future. This capacity of temporal interpretation is none other than that of the transcendental imagination. Ricoeur can thus claim: "What is resignified by narrative is what was already presignified at the level of human acting. Our preunderstanding of the world of action...is characterized by the mastering of a network of intersignifications constitutive of the semantic resources of human acting. Being-in-the-world according to narrativity is a being-in-the-world already marked by the linguistic practice leading back to this pre-understanding. The iconic augmentation in question here depends upon the prior augmentation of readability that action owes to the interpretants already at work. Human action can be oversignified, because it is already presignified by all modes of its symbolic articulation."[52]

It is in his analysis of the configurative function of narrative, however, that Ricoeur most explicitly identifies the role of productive imagination. By narrative configuration he means the temporal synthesis of heterogenous elements—or to put it more simply, the ability to create a plot which transforms a sequence of events into a story. This consists of "grasping together" the individual incidents, characters and actions so as to produce the unity of a temporal whole. The narrative act of emplotment, which configures a manifold into a synthesis, enacts what Kant defined as the productive power of transcendental imagination. As a power of grasping the many under the rules of the same, the narrative imagination is one which introduces recollection and repetition into a linear sequence of events (natural time) thus making it into a recapitulative story (narrative time): "In reading the ending in the beginning and the beginning in the ending, we also learn to read time itself backwards, as the recapitulation of the initial conditions of a course of action in its terminal conditions."[53]

In this manner Ricoeur translates the schematism of imagination from the metaphorical act to the larger scenario of the narrative act. In short, he extends his analysis of the functioning of the poetical imagination from the unit of the **word** (symbol) and the **sentence** (metaphor) to that of the **text** as a whole (narrative). "We ought not to hesitate," he says, "in comparing the production of the configurational act to the work of the productive imagination. This latter must be understood not as a psychologizing faculty but as a transcendental one. The pro-ductive imagination is not only rule-governed, it constitutes the generative matrix of rules. In Kant's first **Critique**, the categories of the understanding are first schematized by the productive imagination. The schematism has this power because the productive imagination fundamentally has a synthetic function. It connects understanding and intuition by engendering syntheses that are intellectual and intuitive at the same time. Emplotment, too, engenders a mixed intelligibility between what has been called the point, theme or thought of a story, and the intuitive presentation of circumstances, characters, episodes, and changes of fortune that make up the denouement. In this way we may speak of a schematism of the narrative function."[54]

This analysis of the schematizing function of narrativity brings Ricoeur to one of the most crucial questions of **Time and Narrative**—the problematic relationship between **tradition** and **innovation**. Imagination, once again, comes to the rescue by operating in a double capacity. Insofar as it secures the function of recollecting and reiterating types across discontinuous episodes, imagination is plainly on the side of tradition. But insofar as it fulfills its equally essential function of projecting new horizons of possibility, imagination is committed to the role of semantic—and indeed ontological—innovation. As soon, however, as one recognizes the schematizing and synthesizing power of imagination at work in narrative, the very notions of tradition and innovation become complimentary rather than antagonistic. Thus Ricoeur can claim that the term tradition must be reunderstood not as the "inert transmission of some already dead deposit of material but as the living transmission of an innovation always capable of being reactivated by a return to the most creative moments of poetic activity."[55] Thus interpreted, tradition can only survive, can only pass itself on from one generation to the next, by fostering creative innovation in its midst. The function of tradition plays a role analogous to that of narrative paradigms: they only constitute the grammar that directs the composition of new works but they do not and cannot eradicate the role of *poiesis* which in the last analysis is what makes each work of art different, singular, unique—an "original production, a new existence in the linguistic kingdom."[56]

The reverse is equally true. If tradition cannot survive without innovation, neither can innovation survive without tradition. Once again we see it is imagination which plays this reciprocal role. "Innovation remains a form of behaviour governed by rules," writes Ricoeur. "The labour of imagination is not born from nothing. It is bound in one way or another to the tradition's paradigms. But the range of solutions is vast. It is deployed between the two poles of servile application and calculated deviation, passing through every degree of "rule-governed deformation."[57] While myth, folktale and traditional narratives in general gravitate towards the first pole, the more modern and post-modern exercises in narrative tend towards deviation. And so we find that the *nouveau roman* becomes a form of *anti-roman* where the very notions of narrative configuration and synthesis seem redundant. But this idea of a total suspension of tradition, in favor of unfettered deviation, is one strongly contested by Ricoeur. "The possibility of deviation is inscribed in the relation between sedimented paradigms and actual works," claims Ricoeur. "Short of the extreme case of schism, it is just the

19

opposite of servile application. Rule governed deformation constitutes the axis around which the various changes of paradigm through application are arranged. It is this variety of applications that confers a history on the productive imagination and that, in counterpoint to sedimentation, makes a narrative tradition possible."[58]

In short, the schematizing function of productive imagination involves both **tradition** and **innovation**. And this dual function of imagination as a poetic creation of the new by reference to the old is not just a property of writing but also and equally of **reading**. Indeed, Ricoeur goes so far as to claim that in many contemporary works of art it is the imaginative task of the reader to complete the narrative sketched out and often even deliberately fragmented by the written work: "If emplotment can be described as an act of the productive imagination, it is insofar as this act is the joint work of the text and reader." For it is the act of reading, which accompanies the interplay of the innovation and sedimentation of paradigms, that schematizes emplotment. "In the act of reading, the receiver plays with the narrative constraints, brings about gaps, takes part in the combat between the novel and the anti-novel, and enjoys the pleasure that Roland Barthes calls the pleasure of the text."[59] Taking the example of Joyce's **Ulysses** as a narrative full of holes, gaps and indeterminacies of plot, Ricoeur concludes that such a text serves as an added invitation to the creative power of the reader's imagination: "It challenges the reader's capacity to configure what the author seems to take malign delight in defiguring. In such an extreme case, it is the reader, almost abandoned by the work, who carries the burden of emplotment."[60]

Conclusion: The Social Imaginary

It is at this final stage of narrative imagination—the reader's creative reception of the text—that the hermeneutic circle returns to the world of action. The act of reading, as Ricoeur puts it, is the ultimate indicator of the "refiguring of the world of action under the sign of the plot." Narrative plots are not, of course, confined to literature. Ricoeur is well aware of this. There is, he recognizes, a whole set of collective stories and histories which need not bear the signature of any individual author, and which exercise a formative influence on our modes of action and behavior in society. This is what Ricoeur calls the "social imaginary." And, as he argues, this "social imagination is constitutive of social reality itself."[61] Ricoeur examines it under two limit ideas—**ideology** and **utopia**.

In his **Lectures on Ideology and Utopia** (1986), Ricoeur spells out the similarities and differences of these two pivotal functions of our "social imaginary." Though both constitute sets of collective images which motivate a society towards a certain mode of thinking and acting, ideology tends towards "integration" (preserving a sense of shared identity) while "utopia" works in the opposite direction of rupture (introducing a sense of novelty, difference, discontinuity with past and present). In the Fifteenth Lecture he explains the basic contrast thus:

On the one hand, imagination may function to preserve an order. In this case the function of the imagination is to stage a process of identification that mirrors the order. Imagination has the appearance here of a picture. On the other hand, though, imagination may have a disruptive function; it may work as a breakthrough. Its image in this case is productive, an imagining of something else, the elsewhere. In each of its three roles, ideology represents the first kind of imagination; it has a function of preservation, of conservation. Utopia, in contrast, represents the second kind of imagination; it is always the glance from nowhere.[62]

In the Eighteenth Lecture Ricoeur elaborates on this distinction between ideology as image-picture and utopia as image-fiction. While "all ideology repeats what exists by justifying it, and so gives a picture of what is...Utopia has the fictional power of redescribing life." Once again Ricoeur combines the Kantian distinction between reproductive and productive imagination with the phenomenological distinction between imaging as a "neutralizing" of perception and as a "free variation of possibilities." On this count, Ricoeur clearly places the utopian function on the side of the productive and free imagination, affirming its power not only as a critique of ideology (insofar as it distances us from what is given) but also as a creative projection of possible social worlds. As he argues in the First Lecture, utopia "has a constitutive role in helping us rethink the nature of our social life." It is, at best, the "fantasy of an alternative society and its exteriorization **nowhere**" which can enable utopia to operate as one of the most formidable contestations of what is.

Every society, Ricoeur claims, participates in a socio-political *imaginaire*. This represents the ensemble of mythic or symbolic discourses which serve to motivate and guide its citizens. The "social imaginary" can function as an **ideology** to the extent that it reaffirms a society in its identity by representing or recollecting its "foundational symbols." Thus Soviet society remembers its October revolution, Britain its "glorious revolution," the United States 1776, France 1789, Ireland 1916, and so on. And non-revolutionary societies may recall their originating myths and legends to insure a similar sense of ideological continuity. This use of a "social imaginary" as an ideological recollection of sacred

21

foundational acts, often serves to integrate and legitimate a social order. It is particularly conspicuous during moments of cultural or political revival. But it can also give rise to "a stagnation of politics" where each power simply repeats the stereotypical images of an anterior power by way of consolidating its status. In such instances, one finds that "every prince wants to be Caesar, every Caesar wants to be Alexander, every Alexander wants to Hellenise an Oriental despot."[63] By ritualizing and codifying its experiences in terms of idealized self-images, recollected from the past, a society provides itself with an ideological stability: A unity of collective imagination which may well be missing from the everyday realities of that society. Thus, while Ricoeur readily acknowledges that every culture constitutes itself by telling stories of its own past, he warns against the ideological abuses attendant upon such a process of imaginative restoration. "The danger is that this reaffirmation can be perverted, usually by monopolistic elites, into a mystificatory discourse which serves to uncritically vindicate or glorify the established political powers. In such instances, the symbols of a community become fixed and fetishized; they serve as lies."[64]

It is at this point that **utopia** as an adversarial visage of the "social imaginary" comes into play. Where ideology sponsored reaffirmation, utopia introduces rupture. Images of utopia remain critical of ideological power. They challenge the consensual continuities of tradition and point towards an "elsewhere," a "no-place," a society that is "not yet." But dangers can enter in here also. As soon as a utopian imaginary relaxes its critical guard, it can establish itself as a new orthodoxy in its own right—its future images becoming just as dogmatic as the ideological images of the past it ostensibly seeks to dismantle. If the social imaginary of a utopia becomes too far removed from the society it is proposing to liberate, it runs the risk of a total schism which ultimately degenerates into repression. It is with this in mind that Ricoeur warns against a "dangerously schizophrenic utopian discourse which projects a static future without ever producing the conditions of its realization."[65] This can happen, for example, with the Marxist-Leninist notion of utopia if one announces the final "withering away of the state" without taking the necessary measures to make such a goal realizable. In such instances, the utopian imaginary functions as a future completely cut off from the experience of past and present—a "mere alibi for the consolidation of the repressive powers that be." Thus, instead of demystifying the abuses of ideology, utopia can serve as a mystificatory ideology in its own right—justifying the oppressions of today in the name of some unattainable liberties of tomorrow. Ricoeur concludes accordingly that the two faces of the social imaginary—the ideological and the utopian—are indispensable to each other. "Ideology as a symbolic confirmation of the past and utopia as a symbolic opening towards the future are complementary."[66] Once cut off from each other, they fall into extreme forms of political pathology: the one incarcerating us in the past, the other sacrificing us to the future.

Ricoeur here rejoins Marcuse's view that all authentic "utopia[s are] grounded in recollection."[67] Critique, he recalls, is also a tradition—one reaching back indeed to the Biblical narratives of exodus and resurrection or to the Greek narratives of Socratic defiance.[68] We may witness this in a genuine theology of liberation, for example, which gives direction to the utopian projection of a future by grounding it in the gospel memories of sharing and in the actual experiences of communal solidarity. The Biblical promise of a kingdom is thus an image which reconnects the future with the past—with tradition, in the best sense of the word, as an ongoing narrative project, as a possibility which demands to be realized. "The promise remains unfulfilled until the utopia is historically realized; and it is precisely the not-yet-realized horizon of this promise which binds men together as a community, which prevents utopia detaching itself as an empty dream."[69]

The same applies, needless to say, to a philosophy of emancipation. To be genuine such a philosophy must seek to bring together the utopian "horizon of expectation" with our actual "field of experience." If the modern idea of progress totally divorces itself from the inherited narratives of tradition and the present realm of concrete experience, it becomes pathologically devoid of meaning. The universal loses contact with the actual. Expectancy becomes dissociated from experience. The **ought** floats free from the **is**. Whereas the Grand Narratives of Christianity and Marxism provided intermediary steps leading from a past of bondage to a future of emancipation, we now appear bereft of such universal stories of historical continuity. "We don't seem to believe in these intermediaries any more," observes Ricoeur. "The problem today is the apparent impossibility of unifying world politics, of mediating between the polycentricity of our everyday political practice and the utopian horizon of a universally liberated humanity. It is not that we are without utopia, but that we are without **paths** to utopia. And without a path towards it, without concrete and practical mediation in our field of experience, utopia becomes a sickness."[70]

By the same token, ideology as a system of pre-established paths laid down by past tradition is equally sick if not directed toward some future goal or utopia. That is why we require, perhaps more than ever, the schematizing function of a productive "social imagination" capable of mediating between these two divorced

23

richard
kearney

realms of past and future. By bringing the two faces of the "social imaginary" together—establishing a creative dialogue between the narratives of ideology and utopia, between experience and expectancy—Ricoeur's hermeneutic enterprise highlights the indispensable role of imagination in the contemporary world. "An urgent task today is to preserve the tension between tradition and utopia. The challenge is to reanimate tradition and bring utopia closer."[71]

That this task of creative imagination is central to Ricoeur's overall hermeneutic itinerary, albeit most explicit in his recent work on the social imaginary, is acknowledged by the author himself in this revealing statement of his fundamental philosophical project:

Despite appearances, my single problem since beginning my reflections has been creativity. I considered it from the point of view of individual psychology in my first works on the will, and then at the cultural level with the study on symbolisms. My present research on the narrative places me precisely at the heart of this social and cultural creativity, since telling a story...is the most permanent act of societies. In telling their own stories, cultures create themselves....It is true that I have been silent from the point of view of practice, but not at all at the theoretical level, because the studies I have already published on the relation between Ideology and Utopia are entirely at the centre of this preoccupation.[72]

Is this not testimony to the hypothesis, observed in our presentation throughout, that Ricoeur's ultimate wager remains a hermeneutics of creative imagination?

University College, Dublin

ENDNOTES

1. Martin Heidegger comes close to such a hermeneutics of imagination in his **Kant and the Problem of Metaphysics** (1929), as does H.-G. Gadamer in **Truth and Method** (1960). However, both thinkers offer more of a commentary on the Kantian theory of transcendental imagination than a distinctively hermeneutic development of it (i.e. as attempted by Ricoeur in **The Rule of Metaphor** (1975) and subsequent works, see the sections on "The Poetic Imagination" and "The Social Imagination" below). I examine Heidegger's interpretation of Kant's theory of imagination in **The Wake of Imagination** (Hutchinson/University of Minnesota Press, 1988, pp. 189-195, 222-224). Other useful and more detailed readings of the Heideggerian interpretation of the Kantian imagination include W.J. Richardson's **Heidegger: From Phenomenology to Thought**, Nijhoff,

24

ricoeur and hermeneutic imagination

The Hague, 1963, and Calvin O. Schrag, **Heidegger and Cassirer on Kant**, Vol. 58, 1967, pp. 87-100. See also Hannah Arendt's reading of the Kantian imagination in **Kant's Political Philosophy**, University of Chicago Press, 1982, pp. 79-89.

2.   Paul Ricoeur, "L'imagination dans le discours et dans l'action" in **Du Texte à l'action**, Ed. du Seuil, 1986, pp. 215-216.

3.   Paul Ricoeur, "Herméneutique de l'idée de Révélation" in **La Révélation**, Brussels, Facultés universitaires Saint-Louis, 1977, p. 54.

4.   Paul Ricoeur, "L'imagination dans le discours et dans l'action," in **Du Texte à l'action**. Ed. du Seuil, 1986, pp. 213-219.

5.   Ibid. pp. 213-219.

6.   Gaston Bachelard, **Poetics of Space**, Beacon Press, 1958, p. xix. Cited by Ricoeur in **The Rule of Metaphor**, University of Toronto Press, 1977, pp. 214-215.

7.   Paul Ricoeur, "Myth as the Bearer of Possible Worlds," in Richard Kearney's **Dialogues with Contemporary Continental Thinkers**, Manchester University Press, 1984, pp. 44-45. See also my "Note on the Hermeneutics of Dialogue" in the same volume, pp. 127-133; and P. Ricoeur's "The Hermeneutical Function of Distanciation," in **Hermeneutics and the Human Sciences**, Cambridge University Press, 1981, p. 139f.

8.   Paul Ricoeur, "Myth as the Bearer of Possible Worlds", in **Dialogues**, p. 44.

9.   Paul Ricoeur, op. cit., p. 45.

10.   Ibid., p. 45.

11.   Paul Ricoeur, "L'imagination dans le discours et dans l'action," op. cit. See also Theoneste Nkeramihigo's discussion of Ricoeur's theory of imagination in **L'homme et la transcendance selon Paul Ricoeur**, Le Sycamore, Paris, 1984, pp. 241-244.

12.   Paul Ricoeur, **The Symbolism of Evil**, Beacon, 1969, pp. 10-11.

13.   Paul Ricoeur, **De l'interprétation: Essai sur Freud**, Ed. du Seuil, Paris, 1965, pp. 23-24. (English translation, **Freud and Philosophy: An Essay on Interpretation**, Yale University Press, 1970.)

15.   Ibid., p. 24.

16.   Ibid., p. 25.

17.   Paul Ricoeur, **The Symbolism of Evil**, p. 12.

18.   Ibid., pp. 12-13.

19. *Ibid.*, p. 13.

20. *Ibid.*, p. 14.

21. *Ibid.*, p. 13.

22. *Ibid.*, p. 13.

23. Paul Ricoeur, **De l'Interprétation**, p. 25. But to say that a symbol is always a sign—or a mode of linguistic signification—is not to say that every sign is a symbol. The sign always stands for something (idea, meaning, object, person); but a symbol contains a double intentionality—it can aim at two or more meanings at the same time. This is evident in the ability of poetic language (to take the paramount example) to have at least "two thinks at a time," as Joyce once remarked. Symbolic images have a literal meaning and a secondary analogical meaning. Thus, to take Ricoeur's example from **The Symbolism of Evil**, the biblical image of somebody being "defiled" refers both to the **literal** function of this image as a sign of physical uncleanliness and to its **symbolic** allusion to man's impure or deviant relationship to the sacred. The literal meaning of a stain points beyond itself to the existential condition of sinfulness which is **like** a stain. As Ricoeur puts it: "Contrary to the perfectly transparent technical signs, which say only what they want to say in positing that which they signify, symbolic signs are opaque, because the first, liberal, obvious meaning itself points analogically to a second meaning which is not given otherwise than in it" (*Ibid.* p. 15). It is because there is no **direct** discourse for the confession of evil that symbolism becomes the privileged means of expression. In other words, the experience of evil is always conveyed by means of expressions (e.g., stain, rebellion, straying from the path, bondage and so on) borrowed from the field of everyday physical existence which refer **indirectly** to another kind of experience—our experience of the sacred. Ricoeur concludes accordingly that symbolic images are "donative" in that a primary meaning gives rise to a secondary one which surpasses the first in its semantic range and reference.

To further clarify what he means by symbol, Ricoeur contrasts it to allegory. While an allegory relates one meaning directly to another, without residue or ambiguity, a symbol works by enigmatic suggestion or evocation—it designates a surplus of meaning which exceeds the obvious one. Allegories have one meaning, symbols two or more.

24. Paul Ricoeur, **The Symbolism of Evil**, p. 18.

25. *Ibid.*, p. 19.

26. *Ibid.*, p. 249. "There is no pure philosophy without presuppositions," Ricoeur argues. "A hermeneutic meditation on symbols starts from speech that has already taken place...its first task is from the midst of speech to remember; to remember with a view to beginning" (pp. 348-49).

27. *Ibid.*, p. 351.

ricoeur and
hermeneutic
imagination

28. *Ibid.*, p. 351.

29. Paul Ricoeur, **De l'Interprétation**, p. 23. Here Ricoeur tightens his definition of the symbolic image by distinguishing it from two competing models, one too expansive, the other too restrictive. The restrictive definition—which Ricoeur equates with the Platonic and neo-Platonic model of formal analogy—reduces the symbol to a one to one correspondence between pre-existing meanings. This relation of proportional correspondence between meanings can be assessed from **without** at a purely intellectual level. It thus ignores the inner creative power of symbolism to generate a surplus of meaning within itself—a semantic surplus which calls for interpretation in order to make sense of the new meaning, a second meaning which emerges from the first (*Ibid.,* pp. 26-27). The "expansive" definition, by contrast, equates the symbolic function with the function of mediation in general—that is, with the function of human consciousness to construct a universe of meaning ranging from perception to language. This expansive model was given common currency by Ernst Cassirer, whose three volume **The Philosophy of Symbolic Forms** was published in the fifties. According to this model, the symbolic (*das Symbolische*) designates the basic precondition of all modes of giving meaning to reality. For Cassirer the symbolic refers to the universal activity of 'mediating' between consciousness and reality, an activity which operates in art, religion, science, language etc. Ricoeur's objection to this expansive definition is that in including all mediating and objectifying functions under the title of 'symbolism,' the concept of symbol becomes so amplified as to refer both to real and imaginary worlds, that is, to **everything**. So doing, Cassirer appears to dissolve the distinction—so fundamental to hermeneutics—between univocal and multivocal expressions. Ricoeur insists, on the contrary, on a strict hermeneutic division between different fields of meaning—the field of signification in general (which Cassirer equates with the symbolic) and the more specific field or double or multiple meanings—where a literal meaning calls forth other meanings. It is only this latter field which, Ricoeur argues, deserves the designation "symbolic" proper to hermeneutics. In short, the symbolic image is one which says something more than what it appears to say. It opens up an indirect or oblique meaning on the basis of a direct one—thus provoking the hermeneutic activity of **interpretation**. Hermeneutics is devoted to the specific investigation of symbolic images which contain "the relation of one level of meaning to another" (*Ibid.*, p. 22).

30. Paul Ricoeur, **De l'Interprétation**, p. 24.

31. *Ibid.*, p. 28.

32. *Ibid.*, p. 26.

33. *Ibid.*, p. 24. Ricoeur remarks here on the suggestiveness of the Greek term *enigma*—"The enigma does not block (hermeneutic) intelligence but provokes it: there is something to unfold, or unwrap in the symbol" (*Ibid.*, p. 26). It is precisely the double meaning, the intentionality of a second sense in and through a primary sense which solicits critical interpretation. It is because dream images involve an internal

27

transgression of one meaning by another that Ricoeur concludes that hermeneutic interpretation belongs organically to the hermeneutic process.

34. *Ibid.*, p. 27.

35. Paul Ricoeur, **Le Conflit des Interprétations**, Ed. du Seuil, Paris, 1969. (English translation, **The Conflict of Interpretations**, Northwestern University Press, 1974), pp. 328-329.

36. *Ibid.*, p. 328.

37. *Ibid.*, p. 399.

38. Paul Ricoeur, "The Creativity of Language," in **Dialogues**, p. 17.

39. Paul Ricoeur, "The Function of Fiction in Shaping Reality," **Man and World**, 1979, 12, 130. Quoted G. Taylor, Introduction to **Lectures on Ideology and Utopia**, by P. Ricoeur, Columbia University Press, 1986, p. xxviii.

40. Paul Ricoeur, **The Rule of Metaphor**, Routledge, 1978, pp. 199-200.

41. *Ibid.*, pp. 207-208.

42. *Ibid.*, p. 303.

43. *Ibid.*, p. 22 and "Imagination in Discourse and Action," **Analectica Husserliana**, (1978), 7:3.

44. Paul Ricoeur, **The Rule of Metaphor**, p. 215, quoting Bachelard, **Poetics of Space**, xix. Ricoeur goes on to quote a further passage from Bachelard (p. xx) later in **The Rule of Metaphor**, p. 351: "The essential newness of the poetic image poses the problem of the speaking being's creativeness. Through this creativeness the imagining consciousness proves to be, very simply, very purely, an origin. In a study of the imagination, a phenomenology of the poetic imagination must concentrate on bringing out this quality of origin in various poetic images."

45. Paul Ricoeur, "Poetry and Possibility," **Manhattan Review**, 1981 Vol. 2, No. 2, pp. 20-21.

46. Paul Ricoeur, "Creativity in Language," **The Philosophy of Paul Ricoeur**, ed. C. Regan and D. Stewart, Beacon, 1973, pp. 122-133 (quoted G. Taylor, *op. cit.*).

47. Paul Ricoeur, **The Rule of Metaphor**, p. 306 (quoted G. Taylor, *op. cit.*), p. xxxii.

48. Paul Ricoeur, **Time and Narrative**, University of Chicago Press, 1984, p. 80.

49. *Ibid.*, p. 81.

50. *Ibid.*, p. 81.

51. *Ibid.*, p. 81.

52. *Ibid.*, p. 82. See also Ricoeur's discussion of the role of imagination in historical narrative, pp. 183-188. Here Ricoeur explores the analogy between narrative emplotment, which is "a probable imaginary construction" and the equally "imaginary constructions" of "probabilist" theories of historical causation as proposed by Max Weber or Raymond Aron (e.g., Aron's statement in **Introduction to the Philosophy of History**, that "every historian, to explain what did happen, must ask himself what might have happened"; see also Weber: "In order to penetrate the real causal relationships, we construct unreal ones"). But while Ricoeur argues for a certain continuity between narrative explanation and historical explanation, insofar as both deploy imagination to construct unreal relationships, he also acknowledges a discontinuity: "historians are not simply narrators: they give reasons why they consider a particular factor **rather than some other** to be the sufficient cause of a given course of events....Poets produce, historians argue" (*Ibid,*, p. 186).

53. *Ibid.*, p. 81.

54. *Ibid.*, p. 67.

55. *Ibid.*, p. 68. Ricoeur's hermeneutic reading of this schematizing-temporalizing-productive power of imagination, as first outlined by Kant in the first edition of **The Critique of Pure Reason** (1781), bears interesting parallels to Heidegger's reading in **Kant and the Problem of Metaphysics** (1929), pp. 135-149, 177-192; and to the analyses of two of Heidegger's most brilliant students in Freiburg in the late 1920s, Hannah Arendt (see **Kant's Political Philosophy**, 1982, pp. 78-79) and Herbert Marcuse (**Eros and Civilization**, Beacon, Boston, 1955, p. 174 *et. seq.*).

56. *Ibid.*, p. 68.

57. *Ibid.*, p. 69.

58. *Ibid.*, p. 70.

59. *Ibid.*, p. 70.

60. *Ibid.*, p. 77.

61. *Ibid.*, p. 77.

62. Paul Ricoeur, **Lectures on Ideology and Utopia**, ed. G. Taylor, Columbia University Press, 1986, Lecture I.

63. Paul Ricoeur, *Ibid.*, Lecture Fifteen, quoted by G. Taylor in his illuminating introduction to which I am indebted, p. xxviii.

64. Paul Ricoeur, "Science and Ideology," in **Hermeneutics and The Human Sciences**, ed. J.B. Thompson, Cambridge, 1981, p. 229.

65. Paul Ricoeur, "The Creativity of Language," in **Dialogues**, p. 29.

66. *Ibid.*, p. 30.

67. *Ibid.*, p. 30. For a more detailed and comprehensive analysis of this relationship see Ricoeur's recent **Du Texte à l'action** and particularly the section entitled "L'idéologie et l'utopie: deux expressions de l'imaginaire social," pp. 379-392. This also means for Ricoeur that a hermeneutics of the "mytho-poetic core of imagination" requires to be complemented always by a critical "hermeneutics of suspicion." See G. Taylor's Introduction to **Ricoeur's Lectures on Ideology and Utopia**, p. xxxiii.

68. Herbert Marcuse, **The Aesthetic Dimension**, Beacon Press, 1978, p. 73.

69. Paul Ricoeur, "Hermeneutics and the Critique of Ideology," in **Hermeneutics and the Human Sciences**, p. 99.

70. Ricoeur, **Dialogues**, p. 30.

71. *Ibid.*, p. 31. See also Ricoeur's adjudication of the Habermas/Gadamer debate in "Hermeneutics and the Critique of Ideology," *op. cit.*; his discussion of Reinhart Kosselek's theory of history as a dialectic between "experience" and "expectancy" in **Temps et Récit, III**, Seuil, Paris, 1985, pp. 301-313, and finally his most recent attempts to reconcile the ideological and utopian expressions of the 'social imaginary' in **Du Texte à l'action**, pp. 213-237 and 379-393. See also my own commentaries on Ricoeur's hermeneutics of the social imaginary: "Religion and Ideology: Paul Ricoeur's Hermeneutic Conflict," in **Irish Philosophical Journal**, Vol. 2, No. 1, 1985, pp. 37-52; "Myth and the Critique of Ideology" in my **Transitions**, Manchester University Press, 1988, pp. 269-284; and "Between Tradition and Utopia," in **Narrative and Interpretation: The Recent Work of Paul Ricoeur**, ed. D. Wood, Routledge (forthcoming).

72. Paul Ricoeur, **Le Monde** Interview, Paris, February 7, 1986.

73. Paul Ricoeur, "L'histoire comme récit et comme pratique," Interview with Peter Kemp, **Esprit**, Paris, June, 1981, 6, p. 165. George Taylor provides a brief, lucid, and to my knowledge, unprecedented summary of the role of imagination in Ricoeur's work in his Introduction to Ricoeur's **Lectures on Ideology and Utopia**, pp. xxvii-xxxv; see also the concluding Notes, 39 and 47 to G.B. Madison's **The Hermeneutics of Postmodernity** (Indiana University Press, 1988), pp. 194-5, where he also acknowledges the central role played by imagination in Ricoeur's overall hermeneutic project. He cites the two following passages where

ricoeur and hermeneutic imagination

Ricoeur himself adverts to this central role: The first is from Ricoeur's "retrospective" text "On Interpretation" published in **Philosophy in France Today**, ed. A. Montefiore, Cambridge University Press, 1983. P. 184:

*The imagination can justly be termed productive because, by an extension of polysemy, it makes terms, previously heterogeneous, **resemble** one another, and thus homogeneous. The imagination, consequently, is this competence, this capacity for producing them in spite of ... and thanks to ... the initial difference between the terms which resist assimilation" ("On Interpretation," p. 184). Ricoeur interestingly remarks on how from this point of view the act of understanding "consists in grasping the semantic dynamism by virtue of which, in a metaphorical statement, a new semantic relevance emerges from the ruins of the semantic non-relevance as this appears in a literal reading of the sentence. To understand is thus to perform or to repeat the discursive operation by which the semantic innovation is conveyed" (**Ibid.**).*

The second quotation is from Ricoeur's text "Metaphor and the Central Problem of Hermeneutics" in Ricoeur, **Hermeneutics and the Human Sciences**, ed. and trans. J.B. Thompson, Cambridge University Press, 1981, p. 181:

Allow me to conclude [the preceding discussion of metaphor] in a way which would be consistent with a theory of interpretation which places the emphasis on "opening up a world." Our conclusion should also "open up" some new perspectives, but on what? Perhaps on the old problem of the imagination which I have carefully put aside. Are we not ready to recognise in the power of imagination, no longer the faculty of deriving "images" from our sensory experience, but the capacity for letting new worlds shape our understanding of ourselves? This power would not be conveyed by images, but by the emergent meanings in our language. Imagination would thus be treated as a dimension of language. In this way, a new link would appear between imagination and metaphor. We shall, for the time being refrain from entering this half-open door."

maria villela petit
thinking history: methodology and epistemology in paul ricoeur's reflections on history from *history and truth* to *time and narrative*

Let us begin by a narrative sentence of the type dealt with by Arthur Danto in his **Analytical Philosophy of History**. Our narrative sentence may be put as follows: "In 1955 the author of **Time and Narrative** published a book of essays entitled **History and Truth** in the series 'Esprit' (close to the review of the same name) by the Seuil."

Now if, in order to complete this narrative sentence, I add that these essays were divided into two sections—"Truth in the Knowledge of History" and "Truth in Historical Action," it becomes clear that I am trying to stress from the start that already by that time—about 30 years before **Time and Narrative**—Paul Ricoeur's concern with history had asserted itself. History here is meant in both of its aspects: history written by historians and effective, actual history, that in which we, as suffering and acting human beings, are involved. But Ricoeur's permanent interest in the epistemological and practical (ethico-political) aspects of history admitted, how are we to understand what my narrative phrase also suggests, i.e., that the bringing together of **Time and Narrative** and **History and Truth** still remains to be done? The attempt to do this does not legitimate itself so easily. First because it is between **Time and Narrative** and **The Rule of Metaphor** that Ricoeur asserts the existence of a close link. So, the foreward to **Time and Narrative** opens with the declaration that "**The Rule of**

maria villela petit

Metaphor and **Time and Narrative** form a pair: published one after the other these works were conceived together."[1] Even leaving aside the author's own statement, the link between these two works is unquestionable. Both seek to answer the challenge to understanding raised by the genesis of new meanings or, as Ricoeur says, by semantic innovation, though on different levels: (1) that of the sentence where the metaphor reveals a new semantic relevance through the bringing closer or the clash of semantic fields normally separated in the ordinary use of language; (2) that of the wider units of discourse represented by narratives which, in effecting the synthesis of heterogeneous elements (situations, characters, actions, various circumstances, undesired results, etc.) by means of an act of emplotment, confer a new intelligible significance on a course of events.

Furthermore, if we go along with the view Paul Ricoeur himself has reached concerning the succession and progression of his works (a view according to which "each work responds to a determinate challenge and what connects it to its predecessors seems to me to be less the steady development of a unique project than the acknowledgement of a residue left over by the previous work, a residue which gives rise in turn to a new challenge")[2] we are led to interpret the works (**The Rule of Metaphor** and **Time and Narrative**) as creative resumptions of problematical residues left in abeyance especially by **The Symbolism of Evil**. In this work, which is the second volume of **Fallible Man**, Ricoeur had in fact already encountered **metaphor** and **narrative** (in particular mythical narrative), but he subordinated them to the question of religious language in its symbolic expressions, and he was not yet able to pick them up thematically as questions.

Let us now return to the connection between **Time and Narrative** and **History and Truth**. The attempt to disclose it is questionable not because Ricoeur never suggested it (whereas he underlined the complementarity of **Time and Nature** and **The Rule of Metaphor**), but because the joining together of the two works conceals a trap if we allow ourselves to employ the easy but fallacious organic analogy which invites us to consider a mature work as contained in embryo in an early one. Such an analogy would be of little heuristic value because, to its detriment, it looks upon time only as a factor of maturation instead of making it to be seen straight-forwardly as human time—time of initiative, work, and encounters. For Ricoeur, the widening of the circle of his contemporaries (in Alfred Schutz's sense) exposed his thinking to challenges and demands that were unsuspected at the start. If he did not shirk them it is because, in a sense, he sought them out by the very way he conceived his philosophical work. In fact, philosophical reflection as practiced by Ricoeur not only differs

34

from the self-centered meditation, but also demands that the various epistemic centers involved in the questions he posed are not brushed aside. They become instead a source of perplexity and difficulty which, by being confronted, help Ricoeur's reflection to advance. It is this progress through already established epistemic centers (those of the human sciences) which characterizes the style of Ricoeur's path of thinking--the odyssey of his thought. It is "the long way," as he calls it, which he does not hesitate to take and which postpones the moment of the reflective return—hermeneutic, not speculative—to the ontological presuppositions of all epistemics, indeed of all questioning. This is also why Ricoeur's way of proceeding differs so much from Heidegger's in **Sein und Zeit**; Heidegger's project is that of a fundamental ontology which holds back or even depreciates the whole field of "positive" knowledge.

Yet, as long as Ricoeur's journey may be, it is accomplished with the extraordinary fidelity to a core of preoccupations and aims which mark his philosophical inquiry from the beginning. I would not hesitate to call this search, were I to describe it in one word, a quest for meaning. This quest is not only alien to both dogmatism and naive optimism but is, on the contrary, inhabited by the conviction that meanings are to be sought after (already by the creative acceptance of our traditions) through difficulties and aporias and in spite of the dangers of error and non-sense which inevitably threaten them. Moreover, as Ricoeur claims in the last pages of the first volume of **Time and Narrative**, it is in relation to the genesis of meaning that the responsibility of the philosopher lies.

Now it is precisely the essays collected in **History and Truth** which bear witness to the fact that in Ricoeur's thinking the quest for meaning is closely allied to the question of history. Indeed, a re-reading of these writings, one inspired by **Time and Narrative**, brings to light some constant features and some anticipations. (1) In them, time is already assumed as a dispersing, spreading force and the narrative as a work of synthesis and composition, thanks to which meaning is brought out. (2) Ricoeur's distrust of the "substantialist" philosophy of history has been patent since **History and Truth**. (3) Finally, Ricoeur's interest in a non-positivistic epistemology of history (of which the representatives for him were mainly Raymond Aron and Henri-Irénée Marrou) is already manifest in his early work, as is his interest in the historians of the **Annales** School.

My first statement concerning the way Ricoeur considered the relationship between narrative and time is backed by what he then wrote to make explicit the value-judgment the historian

makes in order to establish the object of his or her research: "...
in other words, the judgment of importance, by getting rid of the
accessory, creates continuity: that which actually took place is
disconnected and torn by insignificance, the narrative is
meaningful because of its continuity."[3] Further on we read: "The
historian cannot elude the nature of time wherein we have
recognized, since the time of Plotinus, the irreducible
phenomenon of self-alienation, of drawing and of distension, in a
word, of original 'otherness'."[4] It may be said, by the way, that **time**
for Ricoeur has always been marked by the Plotinian and
Augustinian seal of distensions rather than by the Bergsonian
seal of duration (durée). Already in 1952, when the essay
"Objectivity and Subjectivity in History" (from which these
passages are taken), was written, it was evident that for Ricoeur
only a narrative could pick up the challenge raised by the
temporal distension affecting human experience. Also, he
already included, though tacitly, history in the field of narrative, as
he would later state.

But once these melodic cells which render consistent the
approach to history in **History and Truth** and **Time and
Narrative** have been underlined, how not to notice at the same
time the distance separating these two works, not only on the level
of their conceptualization, but also on that of their "problematic"
complexity? It is sufficient to note the difference between the
simple recourse to the rudimentary notion of continuity in **History
and Truth**—even though it was already daring to make a
meaningful temporal continuity depend on narrative—and, in
Time and Narrative, the degree of elaboration given to the notion
of emplotment as the operation which bestows on the narrative its
power of temporal configuration. More basically, such a gap
comes from the fact that what in the earlier writings went without
saying, in **Time and Narrative** becomes the object of a more and
more detailed and rigorous problematization. It is precisely the
case for both the question of time and that of narrative, whose
articulation is the real object of the trilogy. Or, as Ricoeur himself
says when stating his basic hypothesis: "Time becomes human
to the extent that it is articulated through a narrative mode, and
narrative attains its full meaning when it becomes a condition of
temporal existence."[5]

In this new problematic context, the question of history as
historiography is included in that of the articulation between time
and narrative. But this articulation is, in turn, directed towards a
hermeneutic of the historical consciousness. It will be
remembered that this is the title of the last chapter of **Time and
Narrative**. Besides, since in **Time and Narrative** it is a question
of setting up a problematic capable of dealing with historical and
fictional narrative together, subtle distinctions are required if we

are to avoid the reduction of history to fiction, but also so that the question of their intersecting (interweaving) may be correctly posed. As for time (human time), it is at present to be found not only in an initial position, receiving its configuration from narrative, but also in a terminal one, inasmuch as it is still time (that assigned to the listener or the reader of stories) to the refiguring of which narrative contributes. Does narrative not open new ways of seeing our temporal experience which make possible new ways of being and acting?

No less significant is the constancy of Paul Ricoeur's fundamental attitude concerning what is at stake in the confrontation of philosophy and history: the claim or temptation of philosophy to set itself up as a philosophy of history (in the Hegelian sense).

So we read in another essay in **History and Truth**: "I believe it is necessary, however, to have the courage to deprive ourselves of it and to do the history of philosophy without doing the philosophy of history."[6] Or again: "History will never propose to our understanding any thing more than 'total parts' (in the words of Leibnitz), that is, 'analytic syntheses' (which is a bold expression from Kant's 'Transcendental Deduction')."[7]

At present such passages are to be read in the light of the remarkable chapter in this third volume of **Time and Narrative** called "Should we renounce Hegel?" in which Ricoeur notes that it is "the very project of totalization that indicates the break between Hegel's philosophy of history and every model of understanding, however distantly, akin to the idea of narration and emplotment."[8]

So Ricoeur's attitude of renouncing the totalization of meaning—a totalization which would be equivalent to constituting the plot of plots, deciphering the supreme plot, or making any other plot inessential, now appears as more rigorously motivated; that is to say, as the counterpart of the full recognition of the resources of intelligibility proper to narrative which cannot be totally (without loss) surpassed and retained (aufgehobt) by any speculative logic. In other words, it is the narrative alone, and not a system of categories claiming to assume in an atemporal present (that of speculative thought) the totality of the meaning of the historical past, which allows us not to obliterate our temporality.[9] In this way Ricoeur can also say of narrative that it is "the keeper of human time."

Having outlined in a general way the question of history in the work of Ricoeur, I shall now briefly present the methodological and epistemological aspects of the question of historiography in **Time and Narrative**. The challenges and demands which

maria villela
petit

Ricoeur faces at this level of his inquiry have a double origin. One goes back to the methodological orientations of French history and indeed to the actual writing of history by contemporary French historians; the other springs from the Anglo-Saxon debate on the epistemology of history. In my view, it is the fact of taking into account these two different orders of problems which confers an unequalled amplitude on Ricoeur's reflection on the intelligibility of history.

The Occultation of the Narrative in French Historiography

In their works, French historians have left the question of narrative in the shade inasmuch as they confound it with what they mean by "the history of events" *(l'histoire événementielle)*, called also "narrative history." This "history of events" was depreciated by the historians of the **Annales** school in their effort to promote another way of "writing" history, indeed "another" history: no longer a political history favoring individual agents in their relation to well-identified events (battles for instance), but a social history, one which would give a large place to economy, sociology, demography and would rely on the constants which characterize a civilization in its relationship to a specific geographical environment.

Now it is important to note that at no moment does Ricoeur belittle this effort (which could be called non-narrativist) of the **Annales** School, and that, consequently, he does not advocate a "revival of narrative" as does the historian Lawrence Stone. He does not even indicate that this distinction between a "history of events" and a "structural history" is perhaps after all not a major distinction, as Moses Finley points out in his essay "Progress in Historiography".[10] Doubtless because Ricoeur's aim is not that of getting involved in methodological conflicts arising among historians, and even less that of prescribing anything to them, but is instead to reflect on what they actually do. What is more, it is in accepting the practice of historians—in particular the methodological requirements and preconceptions of French historiography (which seemed to most resist his hypothesis of the narrative character of history) that Ricoeur puts the narrativist theory to the test. At the same time, thanks to the attention he pays to the actual work done by the French historians, he takes fuller measure of what distinguishes historical narrative from other forms of narrative; that on the level of the explanatory procedures, as on that of the entities (often collective singulars or societal entities), and of the times which history deals with. It is as if his acquaintance with the least "narrativist" of historians led Ricoeur to increase his distrust of a purely narrativist view of history. So, whereas his reflection aims at disclosing the structural traits which, at the level of emplotment, are common both to historical and fictional narrative, he is not at all tempted to turn history into a kind of "story," and often underlines that their intentional aims are heterogeneous.[11] In that way, during an epistemological discussion on the singular causal imputation and the construction of probabilist models of historical explanation, he writes: "It is for this reason that historians are not simply narrators, they give reasons **why** they consider a particular factor **rather than some other** to be the sufficient cause of a given course of events."[12] In this sense, historians find themselves in a situation similar to that of a judge: "Placed in the real or potential situation of a dispute, they attempt to prove that one given explanation is better than another."[13]

Thus, in **Time and Narrative**, Ricoeur answers, more or less directly, certain historians' fears that narrativist theoreticians might underrate the specificity of history.[14]

Finally, to summarize, it is in relying upon and analyzing the works of those French historians who are the most hostile to a "history of events," a "narrative history"—above all F. Braudel but also G. Duby, F. Furet, J. LeGoff—that Ricoeur makes manifest the indefectible belonging of history to the narrative field. A belonging which, if for a long time it remained overshadowed, is today, thanks precisely to Ricoeur's work, once more being recognized by French historians themselves.[15]

The Question of Narrative in Anglo-Saxon Epistemology

However, if on the one hand the rich French historiography with its methodological bias enabled Ricoeur to give it such a large place in **Time and Narrative**, on the other hand it could not prevent him from noticing that in France the epistemological thinking on history has remained marginal. (The most remarkable exception to this is surely Raymond Aron's "**Introduction to the Philosophy of History: an Essay on the Limits of Historical Objectivity**," which was already taken into account by Ricoeur in **History and Truth**, as mentioned above.)

So, in **Time and Narrative**, Volume I, Paul Ricoeur relies mainly on the English-speaking world to deepen his epistemological thinking on history. Here also the question of the narrative has emerged little by little after a time of eclipse. Now the eclipse was not, as in France, the result of methodological options made by historians, but concerned instead the philosophical inquiry on the epistemological status of explanation in history. This eclipse reached its climax with the publication in 1942 of an article by Carl G. Hempel entitled "The Function of General Laws in History." Mindful of a unitary epistemology of science, Hempel upheld that if an explanation in history exists, it cannot differ epistemologically from that in the natural sciences. It cannot, therefore, escape being an explanation by laws which, as is the case of scientific laws in general, subsume particular cases and, once the initial conditions of an occurrence have been determined, allow revisions to be made.

If I may digress for a moment, I would say that Hempel's attempt is a perfect illustration of what Husserl had brought to light and criticized in the **Krisis**: that in modern times the universal causal style of our lifeworld withdrew and was replaced by what he called "the law of exact lawfulness according to which every occurrence in nature (idealized nature) must come under exact laws."[16] In the light of this Husserlian teaching, we could therefore state that, with his covering-law model, Hempel simply forgot that the events which the historian deals with (and whose causes he tries to determine) are not those of an idealized, "Galilean" nature, but far less "ideally" or far more dramatically, those which concern men in their *"Lebenswelt."* Paul Veyne, echoing Aristotle, describes these events as sublunar.

As a matter of fact, it was rapidly pointed out that Hempel's model was inadequate and too far removed from the historian's actual work, all the more so because Hempel dealt with the question of historical explanation while leaving aside the interpretation inherent to the historian's work and isolating it from the historical framework, from the narrative thread with which historical explanation is necessarily interwoven. For, as Ricoeur remarks elsewhere, "...the historian does not intend to subsume a case under a law, but to interpolate a law in a story in order to make understanding again possible."[17] However that may be, Ricoeur acknowledges that Hempel's model had the merit of giving rise, on the one hand to a series of rectifications which could not but weaken it in order to make it more compatible with the historian's actual work, and on the other hand, to a series of "replies" which in fact led to its abandonment.

Amongst the many works taken into account by Ricoeur, let us mention William Dray's, which separate the notion of causal explanation from that of law, giving the historian recourse to a causal explanation which cannot be subsumed by laws. This opens up a way to an ever more refined reformulation of the question of explanation in history, which recognizes its narrative character. I wish to refer also to Arthur Danto's works on the narrative sentence and, above all, to von Wright's theory of action (action being intentionalistically understood), which combines explanation through causes and explanation through reasons. By discussing thoroughly all these issues, Ricoeur strengthens his thesis that it is thanks to an operation of emplotment that the various strategies and types of explanation in history are held together without robbing it of its specificity, that is to say, without history ceasing to be readable as a story which, as such, must call upon the narrative competence of the reader.

Many other authors, above all those belonging to the narrativist trend (especially Louis Mink and Hayden White), have largely contributed to Ricoeur's endeavor, because they have shown how to link historical explanations and narrative comprehension; Louis Mink, to the extent that he underlined that, in and by itself narrative activity is self-explanatory since it retraces the intrinsic relationship between one event and the other. He also upheld the specific intelligibility of historical knowledge by the distinction he made between three modes of comprehension: the theoretical (that of the sciences), the categorical (that of philosophy), and the configurational (that of narrative).

Hayden White, however, is doubtless the one who goes furthest in the sense of a "poetics of history" by his analysis of the procedures of emplotment brought into play by the great historians and philosophers of history in the nineteenth century, as well as by the attention he has paid to the explicative effects proper to each level in the writing of history, going so far as to detect the ideological implications concealed in the very way each historian casts (encodes) his "data" in a figure of speech (a trope).[18]

Once more Ricoeur's approach to these two thinkers may be taken as an example of the way he approaches the works of others. If he learns a great deal through them, he never abandons his critical vigilance. He reproaches Mink for having detemporalized the configurational mode of comprehension to the point of suppressing its ties with the sequential form which is inherent both to the narratives and to the course of events they "represent." As for Hayden White, to whom he often acknowledges his debt, he nevertheless sees clearly that White's almost exclusive accentuation of the rhetorical strategies of historical writings runs the risk of wiping out the difference between history and fiction.

Finally, after his long, rigorous journey through the epistemology of history, Ricoeur, as already noted, returns to French historiography and gives some remarkable analyses, especially of F. Braudel's *chef d'oeuvre*: **The Mediterranean and the Mediterranean World in the Age of Philip II**. Here he succeeds in showing accurately how (that is, by which **features**) this major work remains structured as a narrative.

The foregoing is a very succinct survey of Ricoeur's approach to the methodology and the epistemology of history in the first
volume of **Time and Narrative**. But "thinking history" for Ricoeur

maria villela
petit

means going far beyond these levels of reflection. As the third volume of **Time and Narrative** demonstrates, the epistemology is itself an essential though subordinate step in a project whose ultimate aim is a hermeneutics of the historical consciousness. Within this horizon, the historical and the fictional narratives assembled are considered as essential contributions to the refiguration of the field of human action and suffering, in other words, to the refiguration of our historical condition. This refiguration has necessarily an ethico-political dimension, a dimension which has always been the *telos* of Ricoeur's thinking on history.

It is here that the question of the interweaving of the historialization of fiction and the fictionalizing of history finds its place, insofar as on the one hand both history and fiction send us back transcendentally to a productive imagination (in the sense of Kant's **Third Critique**), and on the other hand, they both change our understanding of the world in which we live.

It could be said by the way that Ricoeur's approach in **Time and Narrative**, being more systematic than historical, leaves aside one aspect of the "reception" of history: the possible "mythic" use or misuse of history, which a theory of reception should also consider. Such a misuse often corresponds to omissions or more or less subtle ideological prejudices which may already have weighed down the writing of history itself. In that respect we have to talk not only of refiguration but also of defiguration of our human condition by historical narratives. Suffice it to remember that here too a "critique of ideologies" is necessary.

It is more important, however, to note the path followed by Ricoeur in order to return, in **Time and Narrative, Volume III**, from the epistemological to the ontological question of history. He begins the third volume, entitled "Narrated Time," by analyzing Husserl's and Heidegger's phenomenological approaches to time in order to bring to light how first the one and then the other, although for different reasons, failed to ground historical temporality as such.

It is only after this careful examination of these "phenomenologies of time" that Ricoeur is led to consider the ontological implications of historical knowledge. Thus one of the great interests of his ontologico-hermeneutical reflection consists in its being carried out as a questioning back (a *Rückfrage*) from the epistemological to the ontological level, although from the start the latter is never out of sight. As we have already pointed out, such a way of proceeding is essentially different from that of Heidegger in **Sein und Zeit**. Heidegger, in trying to completely subordinate the historical sciences to the existential analysis of *Dasein* and to the problematic of derivation of the levels of temporalization (from

Zeitlichkeit, Geschichtlichkeit to *Innerzeitigkeit*), ended by failing to see the problems posed by history and historical time or times.[19]

Now this lack of comprehension would not be such a hindrance if it was limited to the epistemological level. That is surely not the case. Not only does it affect the comprehension of historicality itself (as an ontological problem), but it is perhaps primarily a symptom of a gap on the very level of the ontology as a whole. An ontology which, even though it leaves room for *Mitdasein* and *Mitsein*, would have remained "radically monadic" as Ricoeur discretely suggests.[20]

This having been said and to conclude, let us glance at the ontological implication of history as disclosed by Ricoeur. The first of these implications has to do with historical time, under the triple aspect of calendar time, the succession of generations, and the decisive question of the document, the trace--decisive insofar as it concerns the dividing line between history and fiction. This third aspect is also decisive because everything that can be put in the category of the **trace** demands that the difference be maintained between present and past. The corollary to this is that the past cannot be assumed *(aufgehobt)* without a leftover in an "eternal" present, that of the Spirit, as Hegel wished; but also that the historian recognizes that his critical inquiry leads to a plausible (because significant) "reconstruction" of the past, which a formula like that of Ranke, *"wie es eigentlich gewesen,"* tends to mask.[21] Finally, the reflection on historical time makes it appear as the coordinating **and**, the bridge thrown across human social existence, between two antinomic times, lived time and cosmic time.

The other major ontological implication of historical time, though linked intrinsically to the foregoing one, has to do with the question of the reality of the past, of the "historical has been" and its "representance" by history. This reflection on the ontological status of the historical past leads to the final considerations concerning historical consciousness. By strengthening the question of the present as open to our initiatives and expectations, these considerations deepen the relationship between history as narrated and our history, that in which we suffer and act, these two aspects of history which have always been one of Ricoeur's central concerns.

C.N.R.S.

43   Translated by Kathleen Bernard

maria villela
petit

ENDNOTES

1. Paul Ricoeur, **Time and Narrative, Vol. I,** trans. Kathleen M. McLaughlin and David Pellauer, University of Chicago Press, 1984, ix.

2. Paul Ricoeur, **Hermeneutics and the Human Sciences,** ed. and trans. John B. Thompson, Cambridge University Press/Editions de la Maison des Sciences de l'homme 198, p. 32.

3. Paul Ricoeur, **History and Truth,** trans. with an Introduction by Charles A. Kelbley, p. 26.

4. Paul Ricoeur, **History and Truth,** p. 27.

5. Paul Ricoeur, **Time and Narrative, Vol. I,** p. 52.

6. Paul Ricoeur, **History and Truth,** p. 43.

7. Paul Ricoeur, **History and Truth,** p. 25.

8. Paul Ricoeur, **Time and Narrative, Vol. III,** trans. Kathleen Blamey and David Pellauer, University of Chicago Press, 1988, ch. "Should We Renounce Hegel?", pp. 205-206.

9. Paul Ricoeur, **Time and Narrative, Vol. III,** p. 204. Opposing Hegel, Ricoeur writes: "The very notion of history is abolished by philosophy as soon as the present, equated with what is real, abolishes its difference from the past."

10. M.W. Finley, " 'Progress' in Historiography," in **Dedalus,** Summer 1977, Discoveries and Interpretations, Studies in Contemporary Scholarship 1, (pp. 125-142), p. 139. "... Improvements in technique seem to me a minor side-issue in this context. So, to a large extent, is the distinction between "Histoire événementielle" and some other kind, whether the latter is called structural or serial or quantitative or econometric. It is either another distinction in technique or a concentration on certain phenomena because they lend themselves to new, sophisticated methods. All the possible statistics about age of marriage, size of family, rate of illegitimacy will not add to a history of the family." This statement links up with Ricoeur's thesis according to which in historical discourse, sociological and economic analyses can only play a role of subordinate elements to the narrative, elements whose function are to render the course of actions and events more understandable. (In relation to this, remember his saying "to explain more is to understand better.") In other words, it is the turning into a narrative, the emplotment, which gives its historical character to history. Besides, the transformations which have taken place in French historiography in recent years should also be noted. Thus, both the notion of **event** and of political history have been rehabilitated in F. Furet's and Mona Ozouf's recent works, though this does not signify a return to what used to be decried as "a history of events."

11. Ricoeur thus underlines his opposition to W.B. Gallie, for whom "History is a species of the genus story," (see Gallie, **Philosophy and the Historical Understanding**, New York, 1964, p. 66), and continues to stress the heterogeneity of the historian's and the poet's or novelist's intentional aims, though for him it also means going beyond this heterogeneity to think the interweaving and mingling of fiction and history both on the planes of the configuration and refiguration of human time by narrative.

12. Paul Ricoeur, **Time and Narrative Vol. I**, p. 186.

13. Paul Ricoeur, **Time and Narrative Vol. I**, p. 175.

14. A reservation expressed by, among others, A. Momigliano concerning the combining of rhetorical analysis and ideological analysis (as done notably by his friend Hayden White), which would tend to make it impossible to "distinguish between fiction and historiography," since it ignores the question of the document or the evidence. (See A. Momigliano, "Biblical Studies and Classical Studies; Simple Reflection upon Historical Method." An address to the section on method of the Centennial Meeting of the Society of Biblical Literature in Dallas, November 6, 1980, Italian trans. **Settimo Contributo**, French trans. L. Evrard in **Problèmes d'Historiographie ancienne et moderne**, Paris, Gallimard, 1983.)

15. See, among others, Roger Chartier in **Esprit** (July-August 1988), devoted to Paul Ricoeur. Chartier says that the influence of Ricoeur's works in the field of French historiography is essential (p. 259). "On the one hand he clears away some of the confusion and illusions existing among the historians. For example, the rejection of narrative history as being synonymous with the abandoning of narrative. On the other hand he allows a fairer estimate of recent discussions (largely false issues), between historians on the theme of the return to narrative." Here Chartier is referring to Lawrence Stone's **The Revival of Narrative**. He adds that "Ricoeur's book reveals that there is no ground for debate since this supposed change (innovation) does not exist. It must be expressed differently and aim at the clarification of the various implications contained in the choice of different narrative formulas."

16. Husserl, **The Crisis of European Sciences and Transcendental Phenomenology**, An Introduction to Phenomenological Philosophy, trans. with an Introduction by David Carr, Northwestern University Press, 1970, p. 53.

17. Paul Ricoeur, "Explanation and Understanding" in **The Philosophy of Paul Ricoeur, An anthology of his Work**, ed. Charles E. Reagan and David Stewart, Boston, 1975, p. 165.

18. Cf. our "Présentation de Hayden White, Une Poétique de l'Histoire" in **La Narrativité** by Paul Ricoeur and the Centre de Phénoménologie, Paris, Ed. C.N.R.S., 1980, pp. 161-181.

19. In **Time and Narrative**, Vol. III, p. 78, Ricoeur questions

maria villela
petit

Heidegger's intention (in **Being and Time**) of setting a foundation to the historical sciences. "We may nevertheless wonder whether historiography has found a grounding in historicality, or whether, instead, its own problems have been simply avoided."

20. Paul Ricoeur, **Time and Narrative, Vol. III**, n. 74, note 25: "Is not, asks Ricoeur, the ontology of *Dasein* radically monadic in this respect?"

21. Concerning the illusion which consists in wishing to abolish the difference between present and past—as if history were not an interpretative and critical reconstruction based on the traces left by the past, we could evoke, as rich in information, Balzac's "extreme" or hyperbolical project (and therefore condemned to failure), to write a novel "The Battle" (Napolean at Essling). "Once you shut the book," he wrote to Mme. Hanska, "you should have an intuitive view of everything and be able to recall the battle as if you had been there." But Balzac himself admits that it was "an impossible book" and he never wrote it. "Too much of a painting to function as a narrative, incapable of assembling two heterogeneous spaces at one and the same time ... as Roland Le Huenen and Paul Perron remark in a study—"Balzac and Representation"—on this failed project (in **Poétique**, n. 68). What is "impossible" even for a novelist cannot but be so for an historian, whose narrative, resulting in part from a "fictionalization," cannot pretend, as Ricoeur says, to be anything other than a "representation of the past," a reconstructed, indeed a criticized past, which could never be given as "present."

serge meitinger
between "plot" and "metaphor": ricoeur's poetics applied on the specificity of the poem

My paper runs the risk of seeming partial, biased and marginal, especially if one considers the extraordinary scope of the thought and work of Paul Ricoeur, since I will view principally the case of so-called "lyric" poetry and will introduce into the discussion considerations that certainly pertain to literary history as well as to hermeneutics and poetics. But here it is a task for me, a literary person, to test, **for my own special use,** the fertile potential of the phenomenological and hermeneutic field that is Paul Ricoeur's for defining and identifying the major literary genres, even though he favored more often the narrative approach--the history and the metaphor in the widest sense of the word--and has approached only in an oblique and unexpected manner the given facts proper to the internal structure of the lyric poem. This is my major concern.

In fact, to establish this specific problematic, I shall have to isolate, first of all, **at the very core of Paul Ricoeur's theoretical writings**, a profound asymmetry between the field of lyric poetry and that of narrative which the turn of the argument tends to curtail, even conceal. To my mind, the poem does not directly enjoy its rightful place. But I would also like to point out that, starting from the vast amount of research on metaphor, on narrative and on "emplotment" *(mise en intrigue)*, as well as on the logical difficulties of time, it is possible to enter into the poem as such.

serge meitinger

I will begin by challenging the parallel frequently established between "metaphor" and "emplotment," rather than between metaphorical redescription and narrative configuration, though both aim at a **synthesis of the heterogeneous.** It seems to me that such a parallelism tends to confer undue privilege on the "narrative," upon which rests all possibility of "re-configuring" time. And I would ask myself to what extent it might be necessary to draw a line of separation between "emplotment" and narrative configuration, in order to allow at least one other mode of temporal configuration capable of producing a kind of structure of time which would be free from narrative temporality and function. Considering more closely the specificity of a poem in light of the upheaval introduced in lyric poetry by the "revolution of poetic language" in the second half of the nineteenth century, I would question myself on the kind of structure of time modern poetry seems to seek. Breaking deliberately with the notion of "narrative" as the stereotype of conventional temporal and fictional structure, the poet, having become very sensitive to the prereflective movements of a living language, tends towards the acquisition, the enacting *(mise en oeuvre),* and the emplotment of a more primitive temporality whose fundamental implications he or she tries to "mimic and replay" in and by his or her poem.

Here is where I would introduce the analysis of temporality set forth by Paul Ricoeur through the three volumes of **Time and Narrative,** and complete it with observations borrowed from the works of Jacques Garelli. This kind of approach—offering the possibility of a **discordant concordance** aimed at an (ever open) synthesis of the heterogeneous—would greatly assist us in limiting and defining what could be a lyric "emplotment" based on metaphorical redescription and tending to "re-configure" time, not according to narrative logic but according to a logic where the invention of extraordinary configurations would be inseparable from a living experience of time.

*   *   *

The strictest parallel between "metaphor" and "narrative" is developed in the preface of **Time and Narrative** (Volume I). It is based on the common capacity of "semantic innovation" proper to two acts of discourse. The "metaphor" produces a new acceptation of terms that it brings together by means of an original "impertinent" attribution that it tries to impose in spite of the resistance of words taken in their usual sense—an ongoing and perceptible resistance in the very core of the "figure" as long as it remains **alive.** Narrative, however, invents a plot which combines the heterogeneous elements, as well as the incoherent ones, of a purely given event in order to draw from it a unified and intelligible configuration.

48

In both cases, the new thing—the as yet unsaid, the unwritten—springs up in language. Here a living metaphor, that is, a new pertinence in the predication, there a feigned plot, that is, a new congruence in the organization of the events. (T.N., I, IX; T.R., I, 11.)

Such a "semantic innovation" really belongs to the "productive imagination" working within the rules that it itself promotes. The metaphor must thus initiate the similarity by uniting terms considered up to this point incompatible and thus to "invent," by a change of focus in logical distance, the resemblance which it does not limit itself to discover. And the narrative must "gather together" and integrate in a single and complete story multiple and diverse aspects or events.

But the parallelism goes even further and rejoins the problem of "reference" or "pretention to truth": "Metaphors," and poetic discourse woven from them, are not satisfied with celebrating the virtues of language in an "autotelic" fashion.

...poetic discourse brings to language some aspects, qualities, and values of reality that lack access to language that is directly descriptive language and that can be spoken only by means of the complex interlay between the metaphorical utterance and the rule-governed transgression of the usual meanings of our words. (T.N., I, IX; T.R., I, 13.)

It is this mode of reference—unusual but effective and pregnant with meaning—that Paul Ricoeur calls "metaphorical redescription"; and from the "seeing-as" thus advanced can emerge a revelation of genuine "being-as" at the most radical ontological level. One can say the same thing about the "narrative," that it "re-describes,"—thanks to the emplotment realized by it and which is a "*mimesis* of action"—the givens and the dynamisms proper to human **action** *(agir)* and "the mimetic function of the plot rejoins the metaphorical reference." However, it is here, in spite of the modalization of the observation, that there suddenly appears in Paul Ricoeur's theoretical discourse a fissure between "narrative" and "metaphor," between the narrative function and the poetic function of discourse.

And whereas metaphorical redescription reigns in the field of sensory, emotional, aesthetic, and axiological values, which make the world a habitable world, the mimetic function of plots takes place by preference in the field of action and of its temporal values. (Ibid.)

This statement, at the very least ambiguous, aims at justifying the undertaking of the three volumes of **Time and Narrative** as a study of temporal values of the narrative and their pertinence in redescribing human action and time. Because of the split that it seems to cause between time and world, between "passion"[1] and action, it raises a number of questions which, for me, are far from being interior. Would that mean, in fact, that the metaphorical redescription, to which implicitly is linked the discourse of lyric poetry, is powerless over time and human action, that it escapes from temporality and the "*mimesis* of action" (i.e., from "emplotment"/*mise en intrigue*), contenting itself with sketching the backdrop of "a **habitable** world"? On the very next page, Paul Ricoeur tries to correct the curious impression left by the passage we have just cited by underscoring the fact that

> ...*metaphorical redescription and narrative* **mimesis** *are closely bound up with each other, to the point that we can exchange the two vocabularies and speak of the mimetic value of poetic discourse and of the redescriptive power of narrative fiction.* (T.N. I, XI; TR. I, 14.)

But, at the same time, the philosopher seems to grant to lyric poetry only the ability of translating "in the mode of elegy or lamentation" the practical field of "passion" *(pâtir)* and not that of "action" *(agir)*, thus bringing lyric poetry nearer to dramatic poetry. And I would then be tempted to think that the separation thus established, between time and world, between *agir* and *pâtir*, does not overcome a certain difficulty, which becomes obvious when it is a question of delimiting the areas proper to narrative and the lyric, or of categorizing these two different modes of re-description of living reality.

* * *

However, the difficulty here raised, namely that of the status of lyric poetry in the framework of a *poetics*, goes back to Aristotle, at least. As we know, there is no room for lyric poetry in his **Poetics**. Possibly because, for him, lyric poetry **is not mimetic**. But to understand such an exclusion, one must define the meaning of the concept of *mimesis* in the works of Aristotle and its relationship to those of *poiesis* and *muthos*. Even though Aristotle has never defined the word *mimesis* for himself in all of the **Poetics**, it seems clear that the Aristotelian concept does not continue the Platonic distrust of the value of truth in every "copy," however ontologically inferior to the model, whatever it may be. It is first a question of a name of action which, like the word *poiesis,* denotes a creative activity working according to rules. The art of writing poems, i.e., works structured according to art—or *poiesis*—requires that the human time and action be submitted to a work of "re-presentation," i.e., to a method of choice and filtration, style and ordering, which allows certain reworked elements of reality to attain the status of aesthestic figuration of reality. And the degree of truth of this "re-presentation" will not reside in the appropriate rendering of the alleged "copy" of a model but in the effectiveness "either inevitably or according to the probability," (**Poetics, VIII**) of the *muthos* thus realized.

The word *muthos,* which can also be translated as "story" or "fiction," here means more precisely the process of "emplotment" which is the very objective of the mimetic process. The principle is in fact that "the plot being a representation of a piece of action must represent a single piece of action and the whole of it." Hence, *mimesis* and *muthos* are inseparable, at least in the *poiesis* that aims at the composing of a tragedy, a comedy or an epic. But then, what about lyric poetry? On this point, if we follow some recent commentators of Aristotle's text, we can argue in the following manner:

*Considered...as the center of the poet's self caught in its contingency and particularity, lyric poetry is supposed to exclude mimetic **distance** which alone allows the construction of an expurgated story: it lacks, in short...the withdrawal of the fiction and that suffices for the **Poetics** to ignore it. In the mimetic perspective, it is nothing less than a hiatus. (P. 21-22.)*

The field of lyric poetry thus seems to escape from the "pair *mimesis-muthos*." (Cf., T.N., I, 32sq.; T.R., I, 57sq.) However, the approach of the "metaphor" promoted by the parallel between "metaphor" and "narrative" summarized above, and the first article of **The Rule of Metaphor** (which Ricoeur, in the footsteps of Aristotle, devoted to this question), will lead us to a more varied answer. In fact, Aristotle himself assigns a special place in his **Poetics** to the "metaphor" even though he does not, in this work, examine lyric poetry as such.

However, in this context, linked to the field of *lexis,* which can be defined in the broad sense of the word as "the production of a text by the selection of words" (P. 22), the "metaphor" surpasses the level of a simple transfer of meaning from one word to another: it is capable of involving a radical rearrangement of the wording. The well-known adage: "The right use of metaphor means an eye for resemblances" does not imply any comparison with any model but reveals that the "work of resemblance" results in the synthesizing and hierarchizing of a glance that "gathers together" a number of elements already present and suddenly makes the "resemblances" appear by the creative selection or combination of certain traits. Such a "production" resembles very closely the mimetic activity linked to "emplotment," and the commentators on Aristotle mentioned above establish the parallel between the two activities.

serge meitinger

*...the metaphor can be described as a process of transformation of meaning which would be, within the language, the **analogon** of the movement of "re-presentation," **mimesis** which transforms a human action into a story, **muthos**. (P. 367).*

We can then consider the procedure proper to "metaphorization" as an **analogue** of the mimetic process. This leads our commentators on Aristotle to view the metaphor as the mediating force capable of giving unity to the act of poetic composing, *poiesis*, by bridging the process which aims at "emplotment" via the *mimesis praxeos* and the work of expression which is the narration of the story in words and meters. (Cf., P. 22.) It does not seem impossible to speak of **metaphorical mimesis**—and Ricoeur has already agreed to it in the quasi-repentance on which he had ended his parallel between "metaphor" and "narrative." What still seems to be denied to the "metaphor," and consequently to lyric poetry, is the ability to end up, by itself, a *muthos*, as an "emplotment." That is due, no doubt, to the fact that we do not acknowledge the possibility of regulating and scaling a temporal happening as does the "narrative."

It is a fact, by reason of their common ability to "reconfigure" time in human activity and according to the same modality, that Ricoeur combines under the single word "narrative" the various forms of emplotment peculiar to tragedy (and comedy), the epic poem (then the novel), the traditional short story, and also historians' history. All these avatars of "narration" tend to represent a "single and complete action," having a beginning, a middle and an ending usually found in the modality of "once upon a time" and whose comprehension is linked to the possibility that the reader, the listener or the spectator has a "feeling of the story." But in doing this, Ricoeur seems to reduce the "reconfiguration" of the time of the human action to a single model of "temporal synthesis of the heterogeneous" (T.N., II, 157; T.R., II, 231) and thus seems to **induce** such a reciprocity between the temporal unfolding proper to the narrative and the most essentially human temporality that he is tempted to describe, and to extol "the circle of narrative and temporality" (that is the very title of the first part of **Time and Narrative**, Volume I). There too is the key to the asymmetry observed and already revealed between narrative and poem. The first seems to have the power of restructuring human temporality, taking it under its responsibility according to the given facts most proper to the being of a person. Thanks to this fictional "refiguration," this latter can understand, reinterpret and redirect unceasingly its living experience of time. The poem, however, would open up less the dimension of a time **rethought** than that of a world described anew but subject to the sole variations of feeling. And, in fact, when in **The Rule of Metaphor** Ricoeur considers, extending the inspiration of the works he comments upon, what could be the internal structure of a lyric poem according to **duration**, he tends to consider the ensemble of a poetic text either as a series of "narrative metaphors," i.e., related to one another according to the temporal outline of a story in progress (one and complete), or he submits himself to "metaphorical mimesis" as the backdrop of a "habitable" world, like a metaphorical web which would structure itself by a sort of internal saturation.

However, following an analysis by Northrop Frye, our philosopher will define at least once, in the same work, the concept of "lyric *muthos*." This is still understood at the level of a metaphorical web whose power of mimetic redescription ends up in a "heuristic fiction" without a sharply defined temporal characteristic; but, thanks to the idea of **mood** borrowed from Anglo Saxon criticism, possibilities of temporalization are suddenly disclosed—possibilities which Ricoeur does not explicitly exploit.

*The conjunction of **muthos** and **mimesis** is the work of all poetry.... According to [Frye]...poetic language, with its "internal" and not "outward" turn, constructs a mood, which has no existence outside the poem itself: this is what receives form from the poem as an arrangement of signs. Must we not say, first of all, that the mood is the hypothetical created by the poem, and that, as such, it occupies the place in lyric poetry that **muthos** occupies of tragic poetry? And ought we not to add that this lyric **muthos** is joined by a lyric **mimesis**, in the sense that the mood created in this fashion is a sort of model for "seeing as" and "feeling as"? I will speak in this sense of lyric redescription, in order to introduce the fictive element highlighted by the theory of models into the heart of expression (in Goodman's sense). The feeling articulated by the poem is no less heuristic than the tragic tale.* (R.N., 245; M.V., 308-309.)

The feeling—**mood**—whose inflections modulate the ensemble of the poem and which, in turn, it structures and truly **creates**, is never the pure and simple transcription of an experienced feeling; the poem does not have, *stricto sensu*, a "noematic" intentional object fixed in reality.

Metaphorical mimesis describes anew the elements ultimately furnished by experience: it has always, as it were, purified them and "distanced" them from all real circumstances in order to combine them in an **experiential fiction**, in a virtual model which allows the reader to "see as if" and "feel as if." Here, it is indeed a question of "emplotment" analogous to that proper to the "narrative" or the "dramatic tale." But there is still for us a question of understanding the specific temporality, since the lyric **mood**, though seeming to do so, does not recall a given fact prior to its

serge
meitinger

enunciation; it has, as a matter of fact, a "now" and an effective presence only in the time of the poem as it unfolds. The privilege granted to the "narrative voice," always recalling and regulating what it states in the mode of a quasi-past, in the mode of retrospection, is once again challenged, because neither for the narrator, nor for the reader or the listener, has an event or a happening occurred before the start of the text. The **said** tends to be strictly simultaneous with its saying and thus, at each moment, preserves the latter's temporal ingenuity.

It is indeed here that one encounters temporality at the level of what the British call the "performance" rather than at the level of the "story" itself, which can always be summarized on the retrospective mode. From this point of view, the living temporality of the poem will be closer to that which is peculiar to a dramatic performance than to the one peculiar to the narrator or reader of a novel. The actors show themselves acting either by their performance on the actual stage or by the performance of the **metaphorical mimesis** giving life, on the simultaneous ontological mode of **being** and **non-being**, of the act and the potency, to the elements that it describes anew. The plot, thus unfolded, invents a whole segment of structural time, "dialectized" by the movements of mimetic redescription assuming the inflections of the **mood** and subsuming itself under it. From now on, it is less a question of a "state of soul" than an "extension of the soul" trying to **maintain** a single line of vision—less a "story" which unfolds according to the ineluctable order of a **before** and **after** than the integrality of a kind of present, both living and absolute, worked by the lacinating and contradictory impulsions of the "now."

* * *

It is indeed the reading and the study of modern poetry, from Baudelaire to the present, which prompts the boldness of such "propositions" about lyric emplotment and the temporality of the poem in itself. Poetic discourse has attained its autonomy in relationship to prose solely because of the progressive liberation of the force belonging to the "metaphor." The paraphrase, the comparison and the allegory, dear to classical poetry, denoted in the form of a poem itself that the impertinent attribution, thus highlighted, should be considered only as a mere fiction and nothing more. Poetry was nothing but a picture of things—*"ut pictur poesis,"* a second-hand reproduction, with the "natural" or the real remaining as ultimate points of reference.

Against the tyranny of conformity to the realist model and the presumption which dictates that the copy should always be ontologically inferior, Victor Hugo and the Romantics reacted by

multiplying *métaphores vives* in their poetry. This way of
transferring to language some aspects, qualities, or values of
reality which do not have access to language that is directly
descriptive but which thus "adopt the whole of real
phenomenality" (using Hegel's terminology), leads to the
accusation of "materialism" since their use of metaphor often
caused the disappearance in the poem of the imprint of spiritual
scrutiny *(crible)*. However, the Romantic poets never made such
metaphorization the very texture of the poem; the structure of
the latter's ensemble remained narrative, descriptive and, in fact,
thematic.

Baudelaire is the first to emphasize the exact quality of the
"metaphor" or the poetic image and he will try to structure the
poem from the event, real or metaphorical. Through the
experience of the "atomization" of self which allows the poet to live
"in such an intensely narrow blending with the world, the poet
does not know whether the world thinks through him or that he
thinks the world" (Jacques Garelli, G.P. 100). Baudelaire
proclaims "a world that narrates itself and reveals itself by non-
conceptual language," that of the "image" *(Ibid.)*. And operating
on this prenotional or "pre-objective" level (according to Ricoeur),
the poet opens up the field of an "ontology of the sensuous" which
finds its expression in Baudelaire by "synesthesia," as in the
sonnet "Correspondances" or the sensual recollections of "La Vie
antérieure." But in doing so, this master of the word does not
content himself with glorifying the referential potency of the
poetical "image" thanks to the absence of ordinary points of refer-
ence--of uniting manifestation and creation by the new reality that
he brings to language.

Instead, he creates a heuristic fiction which is the road to redescription (cf. R.M., 239; M.V., 301) and which, at the same time,
structures and temporalizes the poem. The theme of
"Correspondances" and of "La Vie antérieure" is not the direct
result of reading Swedenborg or Plato. They provide, more
properly, the **mood** required for a "semique" and temporal
unification of the text, i.e., "a sort of model for **seeing as** and
feeling as" created from elements, living but dispersed, of an
"ontology of the sensuous." However, Baudelaire himself does
not repudiate allegory, and frequently organizes his poems as
"narratives." The dislike of the narrative and the desire of seeing
the poem "avoid" (M., 455) the narrative can be read in all of
Mallarmé's correspondence. Mallarmé constantly compares or
confuses poetry, theatre and music by uniting them all under the
aegis of the Idea which he defines as "rhythm between
relationships" and which apparently has the same role as that of
mood analyzed above. He thus hopes that we can treat the
development of a poetic theme as we would a musical one, by

serge
meitinger

regulating time according to a rhythm which escapes the universal progression of a narrative, and that the poem may offer in its entire display a sort of dramaturgy which makes it a unique stretch of time when the spoken is strictly contemporaneous with its verbal production. One need only note that the form of a sonnet, which had been its principal support, often imposes its proper norms on this attempt at an integral, poetical theatricality; the constraints of a formal model had an influence on the dramaturgy selected, and sometimes circumscribed the temporal expansion of the acting action.

Only Rimbaud in **Les Illuminations** dares, even before the Surrealists for whom he opened the way, to allow the web of images, freed from all formal, inherited constraints, to produce and organize by themselves the temporal emergence of a form that owes nothing to the narrative nor to any preconceived textual structure. And it is with this double endeavor (Mallarmé-Rimbaud), of which our contemporary poetics has, as it were, confirmed the ideal, that poetry approaches, in my mind, its most proper essence.

With a single act, we are snatched away from the totality of the world already there and to which we have always belonged; the poem places us suddenly at the primitive moment when time and space can appear to us as about to be born. But, starting from the source point, it aims especially at constituting, solely by verbal means, the traits of a **primary duration** which will not, however, be entirely ours—held together and controlled as a "continual present"—if the distension inflicted upon the mind and soul, by a temporality wrenched from the now, did not impose an "operative intentionality" and the anguish of an "incomplete duration," as well as a costly labor of renewal or recuperation.

* * *

Primitive temporality, of which modern poetry "imitates and replays" the fundamental impulses, is directly tributary of consciousness's logical difficulties with time, as set forth by St. Augustine in Book XI of the **Confessions**. Following Husserl and the work of Jacques Garelli, Ricoeur has placed at the origin of his interrogation of human time, in its relationship with narrative time, a meditation on the Augustinian difficulties as possible openings for a "poetical" practice of temporality.

In fact, in spite of the pre-comprehension that we have of the time we experience by the fact of our immersion in the flow of the world, it seems impossible to define its essence or to measure its movement exactly. Time dissolves when we try to grasp it or to check it under a form, a measure or an idea. The past no longer exists; the future is yet to come and the present is always already. In fact, it is the mind of a person which holds in him/herself, "and apparently at the same moment," these three tensions incompatible among themselves.

It might be correct to say that there are three times, a present of [de] past things, a present of [de] present things, and a present of [de] future things. Some such different times do exist in [in] the mind, but nowhere else [alibi] that I can see. (Confessions, XI, 20, 26 cited in T.N., 11; T.R. I, 27.)

The puzzle is not completely solved but, thus displaced, it allows me to define the only possible **site** where the measure of time, intimately experienced, can be fulfilled for us—albeit at the cost of an explosion of the **now** of the mind, of a *distentio animi* which splinters the consciousness—for the past is actual memory, the present is attention to what is actually going on, the future is the present awaiting or anticipating what is to come. With Husserl, we can talk of "retentions" and "protentions" (as well as attentions) of consciousness. The absence of a link between these different "ex-stases" of consciousness, exploding at the "same point of the present" leads to a **multiplicity** or **laceration**. It is only a "dialectic of expectation, of memory and of attention, no longer considered alone, but integrated," (T.N. I, 20; T.R., I, 39), which will prevent, in spite of different tensions, the sterile splintering of the present, and will hold together the three temporal *ek-stases*. Such a dialectic, however, must be articulated and motivated by a single expectancy or aim *(visée)*, and only an *"intentio"* in the form of an oriented and encompassing tension can prevent the *distentio animi* from ending up in the fragmentation of a series of heterogeneous moments.

Hence, "the moment is an act of the mind," the fruit of an "operative intentionality," which tends to subsume the diversity of tension under one totality offered as a unique span of time, an "extension of the mind," kneaded by an "intention" which supervises the integration of the factors of "distension." But the well of **discordance**, Paul Ricoeur tells us, will never be completely dry.

Augustine's inestimable discovery is, by reducing the extension of time to the distention of the soul, to have tied this distention to the slippage that never ceases to find its way into the heart of the threefold present. In this way he sees discordance emerge again and again out of the very concordance of the intentions of expectation, attention, and memory. (T.N.I, 21; T.R. I, 41.)

In fact, the only concordance that may have a chance to surmount the logical difficulties of time is that of a work of art emanating from the poetic act which realizes a **synthesis of the heterogeneous**.

*It is to this enigma of the speculation on time that the poetic act of emplotment relies. But Aristotle's **Poetics** does not resolve the enigma on the speculative level. It does not really resolve it at all. It puts it to work—poetically—by producing an inverted figure of discordance and concordance.* (T.N. I, 21-22; T.R. I, 41.)

The examples preferred by Saint Augustine himself, those of sound echoing and the verses scanned, then the songs sung, could direct us towards the "aesthetic" and "poetic" nature of the solution to be "invented," which leaves unsolved all the enigmas. The problem thus aired is that of a model for re-configuring time, capable of surpassing momentarily the "distention of the mind" thanks to the operative intentionality that it allows. We have already seen Paul Ricoeur bring forward the narrative model the moment he mentions the *mise en intrigue* or *muthos*. It is now up to me to inquire about the principles that launch a *mise en intrigue lyrique*, a mode of "emplotment" which, without allowing itself to fall into the facilities of the **narrative**, boldly faces the logical difficulties of a three-fold present and the *"distentio animi."*

* * *

Thanks to the Augustinian approach to the problems of time, as Jacques Garelli has noted, we find "in the same unity—the interrogation of time, that of the intentionality of the reader or the singer, and that of the poetic unfolding of the text" (T.S., 100). However, this unity—which we must keep in mind when reading contemporary poetry and becoming attuned to the field of reading that it opens up—would in no way summon either the poet or the reader to the comfort or the laziness of ready-made solutions. The consciousness which discovers the world of the text finds itself suddenly in an unknown space-time and at the price of a certain amount of work; it will have to clear a path, according to an "operative intentionality," whose aim values the structures arranged by the text as well as the ability of the reader to "mimic and replay" according to the fundamental givens of human temporality and activity—time and space opened up by the poem in order to outline its **concordance**. In this perspective, I will content myself to evoke now, according to the widest given facts of his "operative intentionality" (as Jacques Garelli sees it) the dialectic between **intention** and **distention** that is at work in contemporary poetry and capable of culminating in a kind of poetic *Aufbehung*.

* * *

If one can say about the "intentional aim" *(visée)* or *"intentio"* that it leads to a true "emplotment," we are obliged to add, however, that it must constantly protect the unity and the continuity in the face of *distentio* which, in the temporalizing projection of the act of reading, constantly ruptures and divides the flow of consciousness. And as a matter of fact, the analysis of the dialectic between the "intentional aim" and the "temporalizing and spatializing aim" operating in and through the act of reading, as Jacques Garelli points out, primarily accentuates the faults, discontinuities and discordances to be overcome. The *intentio* peculiar to contemporary poetry does not necessarily find itself at a thematic, reflexive or allegorical level; it can emerge from anti-predicative and pre-reflective movements, from the **halo** of the senses in suspense which flow from "metaphorical mimesis" in action.

The intentional aim tends to structure the poem just as would a **mood** or an **idea**, but it is not a question either of a "state of soul" reducible to its psychological definition or to a univocal and translatable symbol—since the ambiguity proper to "living metaphor," caught between the "it is" and the "it is not," between a suspended reference and an "invented" reference, often bestows on the "emplotment" the stamp of an ontological enigma, rendered almost opaque by its extreme singularity. The totality of a poem thus presents itself as a "rhythm between floating relationships," whose intentional aim is to support its regularity.

Although there are "no general canons of construction, nor laws of composition," as Garelli notes, and each poem has its "own, effective reality serving as an irreducible sign of the creative act of the poet" (D.P., 52), I would point out the principal characteristics of dramaturgy, proper to the "poem unfolding itself," that must be assumed by the reading *Dasein*. The initial "take-off moment" of a poem is a rupture and a negation. It is a "de-realization" *(irréalization)* of the world around us, snatching the everyday from time and snatching heavy, use-objects from space. Furthermore, the poem sometimes reflects quasi-thematically this negation or new birth. From this point, as a source, a more primitive time will open up, but according to the game of retentions (recalling either a pure recollection or a world negated by the appearance in the poem of already exploited elements of the poem itself) and protentions (opening up either the world peculiar to the poem or the hope of an afterlife of the world of beings which also exceeds the limit of the text or sometimes a return to the world already negated). Expectations will arise (fulfilled, disappointed or unsettled), as will interruptions (by disappointment, negation or radical discontinuity), and memories (erased, denied or extolled as wealth or nostalgia).

59

The temporalizing "dispersion" which results from the three-fold temporal *"ek-stasis"* proper to the present thus furnishes all the

serge
meitinger

elements of a plot "intrigue" that the reading *Dasein* will tie and loosen by her/himself. Added to the games of time are the games of the world: the act of "worlding" *(mondanéisation)* opposes its singular dimension of "embezzlement" *(recel)* to the temporalizing dispersion. In fact, the snatching from the world already there, or the initial negation of such a world, imply a splintering and a re-rooting of being-in-the-world which allows the *Dasein* to experience anew and magnify its belonging in a "pre-objective world in which we find ourselves already rooted, but in which we also project our innermost possibilities" (R.M., 306; M.V., 387.)

But we have not yet understood a thing about the special temporality of emplotment proposed here. For as long as we have not properly acknowledged the movement which literally "holds" the poem—from its explosive take-off to its resolution in the final silence—like a single area of the present, strained and stretched, worked over by divergent or contradictory stresses, it is destined to be surpassed in a *discordant concordance*. In fact, in spite of the "incomplete duration" that they arrange, we must not be satisfied with reading the ruptures, debunkings, negations and logical incoherences mentioned above, as so many signs of *irréality*, of loss or of *délire*.

The poem fills in the hollows and appeases the longings that it itself has been responsible for arousing; unlike everyday temporality, the poem, because its temporality is controlled by an intentionality operating in the work through the intentional aim, tends towards a certain totalization of being-in-the-world. Its temporalizing and "worlding" movement is **oriented** towards the dialectical and rhythmical totality of a "continued present" which aims at allowing no element outside of its "relief"—whether it be by reason of a disowned memory, or of a quasi-opaque virtuality. The poem thus constitutes a sort of "living experience," inseparable from the "totalizing" reading which the *Dasein* must undertake in order to open for itself an area of primordial time where it can "give itself a real beginning" and submit itself, by a return both destructive and re-creative, to its most intimate past, to the givens, to the traces, and also to the projects which are very much its destiny in the time and space of its own life:

…*the reading* **Da-sein** *must maintain in the folds of its memory— folds that have been denied, rejected, bruised—the anchored recollection, although destroyed, of its most familiar landscapes, of its most intimate feelings.…This experience, lived in time, of the surpassing of the givens of existence and of the transformation of memory, is the movement itself of the poetical* **Aufhebung,** *which, in order to surrealize itself in the realm of the "never seen" or "never heard" or "never known" must fall back on the most* *deeply entrenched experiences of life, to destroy them, to remodel them, in order to project them, free and bold, towards new adventures of being and of meaning. (R.D., 151.)*

There is a question here, through the continuous reading of a text that escapes an exclusively reflexive comprehension, of an "experience of being" linked to a specific work on time. Such a dialectic between the past and the future produces a synthesis or *Aufhebung* which, instead of enclosing itself in the totality of a completed and henceforth perfect being, opens up anew— beginning with uprooted and remodeled foundations from the past thus revivified—a future always to be made and to be explored.

And this "result" occurs not without making one think of what Paul Ricoeur tells us, in the third and final volume of **Time and Narrative**, about the Heideggerian *Wiederholung* (repetition) as a possible modality for a **discordant concordance**. In fact, in the light of the second section of **Being and Time**, it is asked of this "repetition" or "recapitulation" to "re-establish the primacy of anticipatory resoluteness over thrownness and in this way to open up the past again in the direction of coming-towards." (T.N., III, 141; T.R., III, 201.) But, in this second section, let us not forget, Heidegger also joins "the apparent impossibility of grasping and determining the total being suitable to the *Dasein*," to the constant "advance on one's self" which characterizes the first moment of solicitude or care proper to this aforementioned one. (Cf., **Being and Time**, Sec. 46).

It seems evident to me that the opening or reopening of the future *(l'à-venir)* proper to both Garellian *Aufhebung* and to Heideggerian *Wiederholung*, both based on an upheaval of our inherited past whose living elements become *"jet"* and *"pro-jet,"* risk forbidding or postponing *ad infinitum* the totalization of being-in-the-world "pro-posed" by the intentional aim. The very word "discordant concordance" is for Paul Ricoeur that of an aporia yet to be resolved which presents itself as the "typical-ideal of its resolution." The poetical *Aufhebung* brought to light by Garelli seems to remain the proper name of a synthesis of the heterogeneous, dedicated to **Incompletion**, always active and always unfinished, linked to a basically "tensional" concept of truth as presented by Paul Ricoeur in the last pages of **The Rule of Metaphor**.

But this kind of "emplotment," which subsumes a temporal and worldly diversity under the species of an *absolute present* (in spite of its triple plurality), does not seem to me less capable of re-configuring time than the narrative model. This "fable" requires, in order to "be," that the reading *Dasein*—by deploying its ownmost

serge
meitinger

possibilities in an irreducibly singular, even enigmatic mode—
invest the area of time thus set up to its liking. However, the
reader's progression will not occur here according to the **before**
and **after** of an already established fiction. In the crucible of a
consciousness which spreads open *(s'étoile)* onto the text, then
gathers itself together in it according to the inventive dialectic of
intentio/distentio, **before** and **after** rework together mutually—
without allowing anyone to follow any other "story" than the one
of its own live temporality, facing difficulties or enumerating the
virtualities of its own future *(à-venir)*.

* * *

It is because Ricoeur grants quasi-exclusivity to narrativity in the
"re-configuration" of human time or the temporal synthesis of
heterogeneity, that I felt I could bring to light in his thought an
obvious asymmetry between the field of poetry known as "lyric"
and that of other forms of "narrative." However, from other
sources, thanks to Ricoeur's own analysis, we have the right to
speak of "metaphorical *mimesis*" and of "lyric *muthos*" as well as
to link these two notions in a single activity. The "re-description"
of every reality already given, effected by actual
metaphorization—which, correctly starting from the
heterogeneous, "invents the resemblance," thus allowing us to
"see as" and "be like"—is not only capable of "pro-ducing" a
habitable world, modulated by the variations of sensibility, but
also of constructing a **heuristic fiction**, capable of orchestrating
an "emplotment" which deploys itself for us according to the most
primordial mode of temporality. And we have been able to
establish—by referring to the evolution of contemporary poetry
and to Garelli's work (which in my view successfully completes
Ricoeur's thinking on this point)—that the emplotment thus
realized, in the framework of a "living present" and according to its
triple popularity, was no longer tributary to the temporal
organization proper to the "narrative," but rather to complex
relationships emanating from a dialectic between *intentio* and
distentio: a dialectic whose field is that of *Dasein's* consciousness
reading and investing the disjointed textual spaces open to its
totalizing investigation, with its own temporalizing rhythm.

The result has to be, under the ideal shape of a **discordant
concordance**, a **re-figuration** of time and space, first of all linked
to the reader's own abilities. The approach to a poem will partake
each time of a phenomenology of the singular (irreducible to all
forms of *a priori* formalization), or of an hermeneutic operating
simultaneously with the living present according to the retentions
and protentions of a *Dasein* suddenly placed in relationship with
its ownmost existentials.

62 In conclusion, I would venture an hypothesis to explain what I

have labelled a "difficulty" in Ricoeur's thought when it finds itself obliged to define the mode of temporality and internal structure proper to the "lyric" poem. We have seen in what measure modern poetry—starting with Baudelaire—settles, thanks to the emancipation of the metaphor that it realizes, the classical modes of poetic language which are always subjecting the metaphor to a pre-established discursive structure: the "revolution of poetic language," analyzed above, thus tends to conjoin, in a single and unique experience, the two moments of *mimesis* that Ricoeur distinguishes in **Time and Narrative** under the names of "Mimesis II" and "Mimesis III" respectively: the moment of "con-figuration" where the work, by its peculiar, internal framework, constructs a singular model of temporalization, and the moment of "re-figuration" where the reader owes it to him or herself to insert this model into his or her own world in order to modify and enrich his or her own apprehension of time.

In the act of a reading, proper to a modern poem, the two moments are, as it were, fused in a single and unique aim *(visée)* since the "configuration" of time peculiar to the poem is only successfully fulfilled in and through the "re-figuration" activated in and through the consciousness of the reader, and according to his or her own "existentials," by the open-ended dialectic of *intentio* and *distentio*. It seems to me that such a confusion provokes in Ricoeur the same kind of alarm aroused by his recognition of the possibility of the diminishing of the distinctly human capacity of "narrating"—a fear he evokes, in spite of a repeated act of faith in narrativity, at the end of the first chapter of **Time and Narrative**, Vol. II. Do we not, in fact, see certain contemporary texts (like those of Joyce, the later Beckett or Claude Simon), drawing or snatching the "novel" itself away from narrativity to "pro-duce" a **literature** whose mode of reading is remarkably close to modern poetry? From now on, is it not less a question of the reader of such texts reconstructing an order pre-established by the author, than of experiencing in the text itself the fullness of his or her situation as a **being-in-time**—with the enormous responsibility of one who progressively invents the rules of a game that he/she is virtually alone in promoting?

Université de la Réunion

Translated by J.D. Gauthier, S.J.

ENDNOTES

1. The term "passion" here, from the Latin *passio*, appears to carry the double sense of *patio-patiri-passi*: to suffer passively, submit to feeling, allow to happen. (Translator's note.)

serge
meitinger

ABBREVIATIONS USED:

Works of Paul Ricoeur:

R.M. - **The Rule of Metaphor**, Toronto, University of Toronto Press, 1977.

T.N. - **Time and Narrative**, Chicago, University of Chicago Press, Vol. I, 1984; Vol. II, 1985; Vol. III, 1988.

M.V. - **La Métaphore vive**, Paris, Seuil, 1975.

T.R., I, II, III - **Temps et Récit, Tomes I, II, III**, Paris, Seuil, 1983, 1984, 1985.

Works of Jacques Garelli:

G.P. - **La Gravitation poétique**, Paris, Mercure de France, 1966.

R.D. - **Le Recel et la Dispersion**, Paris, Gallimard, 1978.

T.S. - **Le Temps des Signes**, Paris, Klincksieck, 1983.

D.P. - "Discontinuité poétique et énergétique de l'être," **La Liberté de l'Esprit**, No. 14, hiver 1986-1987, Paris.

P. - **La Poétique** d'Aristote, traduction et commentaires de Roselyne Dupont-Roc et Jean Lallot, Paris, Seuil, 1980.

M. - **Œuvres complètes** de Mallarmé, Paris, La Pléiade, Gallimard, 1945.

Poetics - **The Poetics**, Loeb Classical Library, Cambridge, Mass., Harvard University Press, 1932.

t. peter kemp
toward a narrative ethics: a bridge between ethics and the narrative reflection of ricoeur

Introduction

The primary intention of this essay is to show narration to be indispensable to ethics in the philosophy of Paul Ricoeur. This is a dangerous project, for when one looks at his recent writings on ethics it is not at all clear that Ricoeur is in fact moving in the direction of seeing narration play a role with respect to ethics. But I believe I have succeeded in demonstrating elsewhere[1] that, nevertheless, Ricoeur's reflections on the prefiguration and refiguration of narration do imply an ethical form of thought. By his own account, the day-to-day life which constitutes the background of the narrative representation is filled with the approval and disapproval of human acts, and the reading of a narrative obliges the reader to take a position with respect to ethics or the vision of the good life which the work, at least implicitly, suggests.

But in his published expositions directly concerned with ethics, Ricoeur is hesitant to take a step toward a narrative understanding of ethics. The reason for this, it seems, is that while he does not believe a moral law in the Kantian sense to be the fundamental principle of ethics, he is nevertheless concerned about such a principle, which he believes can, and also should, be conceived as an abstract rule and not as a narrative. For otherwise, he thinks, we would have no criterion for distinguishing between good and bad narratives.

The principle Ricoeur sees as primary in this regard is the **Golden Rule**: "Do unto others as you would have them do unto you" or, in its negative form: "Abstain from doing unto others...." In a debate in which we have been engaged in the Scandinavian reviews **Res Publica** and **Slagmark**, Ricoeur has in fact suggested "that it is the affinity of certain narratives with the Golden Rule that gives them their moral force," and that this view "preserves the non-narrative specificity of the commandment which prohibits violence and recommends submission."[2] It is true that one recognizes that the **relation** of the narrative converts the imperative into a "vision related from the good life."[3] But this does not change Ricoeur's idea that the imperative of the Golden Rule precedes the narrative being related.

It is my intention to show now that the idea of a narrative foundation of ethics does not exclude the idea of an ethical principle which is both fundamental and universal. I suggest in effect that this principle, which is clearly distinct from a moral law in the Kantian sense, can only be conceived in the form of a *habitus* principle in the Aristotelian sense, that is, as a principle of a **fundamental ethical attitude**. I demonstrate that this attitude actually expresses itself only through our narrative competence in understanding our own actions and sufferings.

In this way, I hope to be able to overcome the apparent contradiction in Ricoeur which allows that the imperative be submitted to ethical questioning (in the criticism of Kantian moralism), while supposing its primacy (in the assertion that the Golden Rule precedes ethical narratives).

But what is required first is a summary of Ricoeur's conception of ethics.

RICOEUR'S ETHICS: A NON-NARRATIVE PRESENTATION

(1) Ethical Intention

Let us consider in particular Ricoeur's conception of ethics as he presents it in his article, "Avant la loi morale: l'éthique,"[4] as well as some of his reflections concerning the Aristotle-Kant opposition in his essay "La raison pratique."[5]

Ethics, says Ricoeur in his essay, "The Problem of the Foundation of Moral Philosophy," is born of a project in which the human being wants to take a stand with regard to her/himself, to affirm her/

himself as free. At the root of ethics there is however an **ethical intention**, which "precedes, in order of primacy, the notion of moral law." By this intention, freedom tears itself away from nature and its laws in order to "**attest** or render witness to itself by means of works in which it makes itself objective."[6]

Now this point of departure for ethics does not yet constitute ethics *per se*. What more is required is "the **dialogical** position of freedom in the second person."[7] To the act of tearing away is added that of **releasing**, which aims to break the bonds which hold the other. In referring to "Emmanuel Lévinas's fine analyses concerning the human face," Ricoeur considers the tacit message of the face more as a request than as a prohibition: the request to love the other as oneself rather than the interdiction not to kill him or her. Citing Lévinas, who says: "I am the hostage of the other," Ricoeur underlines "that the recognition of the face of another constitutes a veritable departure, a completely original commencement, on the ethical way."[8] But despite the primordial fact of ethics being the encounter with the face of the other, the affirmation of my own liberty nevertheless precedes, in the order of understanding, the affirmation of the freedom of the other. This is so since "were I not to understand that which wants to say I, I would not know that the other is I for himself, though free like myself."[9] From this Ricoeur concludes that "all of ethics is born of this redoubling of the task of which we are speaking: to bring it about that the freedom of the other is similar to my own."[10] It follows that "all that is negative about the interdiction proceeds from this positive aspect of the **recognition** via which different freedoms want to render themselves analogous to one another through the medium of responsible action."[11] He adds, however, that the interdiction also presupposes the possible opposition of one freedom against another, and that one might all the same think, with Hegel, that the recognition is obtained only after a confrontation has occurred between different freedoms in the sphere of action and after the experience of crime.

Nevertheless, all ethical intention "arises in the context of a situation which is already **ethically** delineated."[12] It is structured by the choices, the preferences, the evaluations which have already taken place and which have crystallized themselves in **causes** to be defended, ideas to be realized, tasks to be performed; in sum, in **values** which play the role of **rules of action**. One thus passes from the personal sphere where I relate to **you**, to an impersonal and neutral sphere which has the appearance of being already given, and valid with respect to all new choices. This is the sphere of the institution in which what is instituted is a network of moral rules.

(2) The Moral Law

I shall not pause long over Ricoeur's magisterial analyses of the quasi-objectivity of values, analyses formed in the wake of Jean Nabert's reflections on value in his **Elements for an Ethic** (trans. 1969). Let it only be noted that values such as justice, brotherhood, equality, etc. express the fact that the human subject at the same time receives ethics in the form of given morals, and puts this into practice through his or her correct evaluations, preferences and decisions.

These values come half way towards the institution of norms and moral laws. According to Ricoeur, the rule of action takes the form of a **norm** from the moment the human being is divided "half way between a **preferable**, which is already objectified, and a **desirable**, which is closed upon some egotistical interest." "Then," he says, "the **you must** begins to impose itself, which is the height of neutrality, as a rule become estranged from my project of freedom and even from my intention to recognize the liberty of the other. The origin of ethics ... is quite simply lost; here begins the severity of **moralism**."[13]

But the interdiction that value imposes in the divide between that which one has preferred on the basis of deliberation and that which one desires spontaneously is not a simple repression of human life. It is first "an aid, a support, to assure, in the intermittency of desires, the continuity of the moral person," for "the function of the interdiction is to make values safe from the arbitrariness of each of us."[14]

In order for the interdiction to become truly repressive, that is, to become a social repression, it is necessary that it become instituted as a moral law which provides authority in the Kantian manner, i.e., as though it were a natural law. The idea of law in effect makes the thought of order prevail.

In this way the interdiction which was last in the ordering of the constitution of the ethical life becomes the very first, the foundation of all ethics. The imperative which leads to the questioning of ethics in order to protect communal life has simply become its basis. It is this, according to Ricoeur, that is the fault of Kantianism.

In his essay on "practical reason" he makes this criticism of Kant more precise. The greatness of Kant, according to Ricoeur, is his having conceived of freedom as a personal autonomy (something no Greek thinker succeeded in doing) and practical reason as "a determination of freedom."[15] However, Kant wanted to coalesce freedom and law in thought, in such a way that ethics becomes a morality in "strict conformity with its coming to have no concern for desire."[16] This has resulted in a series of dichotomies fatal to the very notion of action: "Form versus content, practical law versus moral maxim, becoming versus desiring, imperative versus happiness," and Ricoeur declares that here "Aristotle renders a better account of the specific structure of the practical order, when he forges the notion of deliberative desire, joining legitimate desire and just thought in his concept of *phronesis*."[17]

Now what Ricoeur considers most deserving of criticism "is the very project of constructing the **Critique of Practical Reason** on the model of the **Critique of Pure Reason**, of seeing the separation of the *a priori* and the empirical as a methodological separation."[18] Thus Kant puts himself "on the path of the most dangerous idea of all, as has been recognized by distinguished thinkers from Fichte to Marx, namely that of taking the practical order to be justifiable on an epistemological or scientific basis, comparable to that required in the theoretical order."[19] From this stems the fatal idea that there is a science of morals in which a moral reason operates that can articulate itself as a critique of *praxis* in the concrete ethical life of the society.

RICOEUR'S NARRATIVE REFLECTION: THE PREFIGURATION OF NARRATION IN THE WORLD OF ACTION

We have seen that Ricoeur, in the articles cited, presents his idea of ethics without the least reference to his reflections elsewhere on the indispensable role narration plays in understanding human time and thereby the human action which presupposes it. But is it possible to conceive of ethics as a questioning which in the beginning is structured abstractly in the relations between myself, you and a third person, only to be subsequently grafted on the time recounted by our actions? Are ethics and the life being related originally two completely separate things?

Recall Ricoeur's description, in **Time and Narrative**, of the living world in which the narrative composition finds its anchorage. This world of recountable events, according to Ricoeur himself, is truly an ethical world.

First it is a world of action, and not a merely physical world. In this world, Ricoeur says, to act is always to act "with" others in the form of cooperation, competition or strife. This is why he declares that, between narrative understanding and moral understanding, there is "at the same time a relation *[rapport]* of **presupposition** and a relation of **transformation**."[20] For, on the one hand, "every narrative presupposes a familiarity with terms such as agent, goal, means, circumstance, help, hostility, cooperation, conflict, success, failure, etc., on the part of its narrator and any listener.... On the other hand, narrative is not limited to making use of our familiarity with the conceptual network of action. It adds to it **discursive** features which distinguish it from a simple succession of action sentences. These features...are syntactic features, whose function is to engender the composing of modes of discourse worthy of being called narratives, whether it be a question of historical or fictional narrative."[21] In short, the narrative is constituted by the plot [intrigue] which transforms the paradigmatic order of daily action into the syntactic order of literature or history.

Second, it is a world in which action is always already articulated in signs, rules and norms. These are the "cultural codes" which, in the form of "programmes" of comportment, give form, order and direction to life. It is as a function of these norms—customs or manners—which are immanent to a culture, that one can judge actions according to a moral scale of preference.

Ricoeur refers here to a work of James M. Redfield who, in **Nature and Culture in the Iliad**, interprets the tragedy of Hector in the light of Aristotle's **Poetics**. This theory presupposes the idea of good and bad characters (ethical qualities) where it refers to tragedy as "an imitation of personages better than the ordinary man,"[22] as compared to comedy, which makes "its personages worse ... than the men of the present day."[23] The Aristotelian interpretation Redfield applies to the **Iliad** makes it appear that "tragedy is an inquiry into the strengths and weaknesses of a culture,"[24] thus, an inquiry into its ethical experience and its ideas of happiness and excellence. Tragedy appears as an inquiry which offers us a lesson on the value of culture.

Thus we find in Homer's grand narration on the fall of Troy a pre-understanding of the world of action without which tragedy does not make sense. The tragic narrative "imitates" the already established ideas of a culture, not only its general ideas concerning suffering and action, but also its more particular ideas concerning actions which are admired and scorned. Ricoeur concludes that the moral pre-understanding of narrative includes a **competence** to use the conceptual network in a meaningful way, as well as a **moral preference**, articulated by symbols, for rules and norms.

Finally, Ricoeur claims that the world of ethical action contains temporal aspects "that call for narration."[25] It is a question of the way in which daily *praxis* **orders**, relatively to one another, what Augustine calls the present of the future, the present of the past and the present of the present. Since that time, one has been able to recount one's life starting from the present of the present, like

Augustine, or from the present of the future, as Heidegger has done in conceiving being-for-death or **anxiety** as that which fundamentally constitutes temporality.

We see that, following Ricoeur himself, we are not permitted to affirm that ethics, any more than poetic narrative, be seen in a completely non-narrative way. But is it only a question of an "inchoate narrative" or of a "pre-narrative structure of experience" as he affirms?[26] I have raised this problem in the paper mentioned above.[27] There I ask whether it is not necessary to recognize that, prior to any artistic composition, people recount their lives and explain themselves to one another by way of small everyday stories, and that if we are able to speak of human life as of a story in its nascent state, is it not precisely by means of all these small stories that this life becomes a true story, a time recounted? I therefore posed the following question to Ricoeur: Would the narratives of historians and poets never be composed if, in the only world of action, there were only "stories not yet told,"[28] or if one were only acquainted with human lives which "deserve to be told"?[29] In taking up this question again I propose now to go further than Ricoeur and maintain that, in the whole of human experience of life and action, narrative structures are already present.

THE NARRATIVE QUALITY OF THE REAL WORLD

I will here refer to a work by David Carr, **Time, Narrative and History**, which appeared in 1986. Obtaining support from the works of the literary critic Barbara Hardy and the philosopher Frederick A. Olafson, Carr maintains the idea that original experience (in Husserl's sense) of time, action and the connection of life does not require literary or historiographical narrative in order to be understood as an experience of narrative structures; he believes that to understand life, *Die Lebenswelt*, is already to recount it.

Carr recalls that, according to Husserl's analyses of temporality, time appears phenomenologically like a melody—not, he says, in Bergson's sense, like a pure river of duration, but as something having structure, indicated by the protentions and retentions of which Husserl speaks. In this way, everything that happens in time has a before and an after, i.e., a genesis which precedes it, something—the middle—which happens, and an end which follows it.

Carr also sees the way in which we hear the ticking of a clock as a *tick-tock* to be a demonstration of the distinction which we force, in the case of a physically monotonous sequence of the passage of time, between a beginning (tic) and an end (toc).[30] And he

t. peter kemp

concludes that we have no experience of time without a narrative configuration.

As regards our actions, they are effected in temporal phases; instructed by the lesson of our experience of the past, we utilize the means of the present to attain an end in the future. The action is carried by a project, an *Entwurf* as Heidegger calls it.

Now if all action which takes place in time is something which begins and ends, it characterizes itself in the same way as a narrative; there is a point of departure and a point of arrival and between the two a middle, the event itself. This structure belongs to the action "whether or not a story, in the sense of a literary text, is told about them at all."[31] We also "recount" this structure—at least to ourselves—in the case where we are both the narrator and the only listener. This is why Carr can say, in opposition to Louis O. Mink who declares that narratives are not lived but told, that the narratives "are told in being lived and lived in being told."[32] In being the agent of my own life, I am its proper narrator and there is at least one listener: myself. Thus Carr considers Alasdair MacIntyre justified where, in **After Virtue**,[33] he asserts against Mink that "stories are lived before they are told."

It is in conceiving of our lives as narrative structures from the time we first assume consciousness that we succeed in giving them coherence. As concerns more elaborate narratives, which we call fiction and the history of facts, Carr emphasizes that they do not transform non-narrative chaos into a narrative order, but that they only prolong the primitive practice of narration, "focusing their attention in certain directions and orienting their actions toward certain goals."[34]

Now Carr does not limit his reflections solely to the passage of time and the unfolding of isolated actions. He also considers the way in which we represent what Dilthey calls "the connection of life"—*der Zusammenhang des Lebens*—which we experience in a sort of reflection or "consciousness"—*Besinnung*.

Here Carr refers once again to Husserl, who, in paragraph 37 of his **Méditations Cartésiennes** remarks that the ego "constitutes itself for itself, so to speak, in the unity of a *Geschichte*."[35] This idea is taken up again by the Husserl scholar Wilhelm Schapp, who has developed a whole philosophy around the theme: "The narrative/story [*die Geschichte*] represents man."[36] But the idea already appears in MacIntyre who—at the basis of ethics—finds personal identity or "the unity of a life" constituted by the coherence of a **life story**.

But this idea of a person's life as being wholly a narrative, a story which commences at one time and is going to end at another, causes problems to the extent that we have not had the experience of our own births nor, in the midst of our lives, the experience of our own deaths. Carr finds a response to this difficulty at the end of Heidegger's **Being and Time**, where it is precisely a question of Dilthey's "connection of life." According to Heidegger, we are in effect capable of thinking of our *Dasein* as a unity with a beginning and an end, if we understand this existence as a being-for-death, that is, as a whole which is limited by its finitude. Thus, says Carr, the existential authenticity favored by Heidegger is nothing other than the will to take on oneself the burden of being the **story teller** of one's own life. He concludes that the narrative coherence of life is not a given but a task, or even a struggle, to bridge the gaps between my actions, and to constitute myself—and preserve myself—as my *Selbst*.[37]

THE NARRATIVE BASIS OF ETHICS

Carr's analyses are a useful corrective and show us clearly that the living world of action which prefigures the compositions of narratives is neither thinkable nor livable without the experience of narrative structures. Now it is certainly in this world that the ethics of which Ricoeur is speaking constitutes itself—to know the dialogical intention between "I" and "you" and, as a consequence, to know the values and norms for evaluating and regulating actions.

It follows that there is no ethics without there being a world imprinted by narrative structures. What then is the relation between ethics and narrative?

Let us return to the definition of ethics which, according to Ricoeur, is born of the recognition of the freedom of others as being similar to my own. He refers to Lévinas, who describes the experience of the face of the other as a demand for recognition and assistance. But can we limit ethics to the pure reciprocal relation between two freedoms?

That would without doubt be a formidable reduction. In order to judge it, let us see how Jean-Paul Sartre lays it open—which he does moreover in a very suggestive manner—in his posthumous **Morale**, written at the end of the 1940s. He gives the example of a person who is chasing a bus and whom another helps jump onto the already moving vehicle. Here the one "sees the concrete freedom of the other,"[38] willing in this way the pure recognition that: "To will that a value realize itself not because it is mine, not because it is a value, but because it is a value for someone on earth...that is to posit that in any case freedom is more highly valued than non-freedom."[39] In this situation, the one makes appeal to the other, and in this appeal, says Sartre, there is a giving of oneself—the appeal expresses generosity. The other, for his part, accepts this help as another free act, and "when the two hands clasp," he realizes "the unity of two freedoms in a single perception."

There is undoubtedly progress here in the study of ethics. Note also that this thought is constructed around a scene, the narrative of the bus testifying to the dialectic of giving--between call and help. Sartre has not created an ethics without narrative. Although, as Ricoeur rightly observes, the idea of autonomous freedom which Kant was the first to consider the basis of a rational ethics, "could not have been conceived by any Greek thinker." This does not mean, as Ricoeur himself underlines, that the Greek philosophers, including Aristotle, knew nothing about ethics, nor that one cannot or should not correct Kant with the help of Aristotle.

Neither Kant nor Sartre has forgotten the ethical intention of which Ricoeur is speaking, but something which can be found in Aristotle has disappeared in Kant and such existential philosophers as Sartre. What has disappeared is the idea of **the good life**, which is realized by a *habitus*, a way of living not only in the situation of the instant, but in the unity of a lifetime. The price of the existentialist reflection on ethics is the impoverished reduction it provides, as though the ethical identity of a whole life does not count for the human being and the life of the community.

This is why one must appreciate MacIntyre's effort to revitalize the Aristotelian idea of ethics in terms of the good life. Aristotle declares, in his **Nichomachean Ethics**,[41] that "one swallow does not make a summer, nor does one day: and so too one day, or a short time, does not make a man blessed and happy." It is this conception that MacIntyre turns to in speaking about "the good of a human life conceived as a unity."[42] Now to conceive of and evaluate life as a whole is not possible, he says, other than with the help of the concept of a **self** "whose unity resides in the unity of a narrative which links birth to life to death as narrative beginning to middle to end."[43] Thus, "narrative history of a certain kind turns out to be the basic and essential genre for the characterization of human actions."[44]

However, "the story of my life" is not a pure invention of the isolated individual. It is always, he says, "embedded in the story of those communities from which I derive my identity."[45] Here, too, we see an Aristotelian idea for, as we know Aristotle's ethics stem from his politics. According to MacIntyre, "the good life for man" is attained precisely by a social **practice**, which in a narrative order realizes its benefits according to certain norms of virtue or excellence in conformity with a tradition.[46]

MacIntyre's work permits us to advance a step further towards the comprehension of the basis of ethics. For if ethics is a particular vision of the good life, and if a single action does not as such fill the conditions for expressing the good life, the result is that Carr's simple conception of a narrative structure does not suffice to constitute ethics. That all our acts possess a certain narrative form is certainly a necessary condition, but not a sufficient one, for constituting an ethical vision. What more is required is a true narrative, that is, a mimetic configuration where the middle between the beginning and the end is not only an occurrence, but the figuration of a **point** which, like "mimesis," **reveals** more than **reflects** a difference between the good and the bad, and, more fundamentally, creates the vision of the good life, as distinct from a wasted and frustrated life.

Ethics presupposes this form of true narrative that Ricoeur analyzes in **Time and Narrative**, that is to say, the intrigue of fiction or historiography. So the narrative can impose itself as an **ethical model**, i.e., as a paradigm which in practice orients life; and it is by this institution of a narrative as a model of the good life that the ethical understanding and orientation of daily action begins. One judges, acts and projects in the light of the narrative in which one lives. As expressed, for example, by John Dominique Crossan, one can live "in the parables" of Jesus, since the parable imposes itself as "the House of God";[47] and the Kingdom of which Jesus proclaims the advent demands "decision and response, life and action, but never articulating such action in detail within the parables themselves."[48]

Ethics establishes itself nevertheless, however, since Carr mentions more elaborate narratives which direct attention to certain ends. A pure narrative structure does not have this function. In saying this, we are not doing the same as Carr, for the point of his book is not to show the basis of ethics, but the basis of historiography. This is why, in opposition to a certain factual positivism, he insists on the narrative nature of all historical life. This consideration concerns us to the extent that ethics appears in this historical life. We stress only that ethics does not establish itself without an elevation of the narrative to the level of the true story.

David Carr is of further significance to us, for he insists that the elaboration of the connection of life is a task of the narrating individual, who is seeking to compose the unity of his or her life like a story. What he defines by this is the **ethical** task that consists in practicing the good life. It is true that the story one composes to guide this practice is an unwritten narrative to the extent that no biography which extracts a structure from it can drain it of its contents. But it must be added that this effort to tell one's own life as a unity cannot realize itself other than within a narrative tradition constituted by the narrative models of the good life.

The point at which I hesitate to follow Carr is where he returns to the Heideggerian idea of the being-for-death as a to-be-able-to-be-a-whole *[Ganzseinskönnen]* in order to have a conception of the unity of life. Instead of considering, with Heidegger, that the anticipation of my own death constitutes the definitive end of my story, what is required is perhaps rather to conceive of this end as a limit, which is real of course, but which is nevertheless surmountable in a certain sense.

It is true that Carr recognizes, as does MacIntyre, that my story is inserted in the stories of others, to become part of a historical world which not only precedes me as a remembered tradition, but which can furthermore revive my story, pursue my efforts and thereby make my life a contribution, beside those of others, to the creation of the unity of a common story. But Carr endeavors to establish a parallel between the anticipated end of Heidegger's *Dasein* and the end pursued by an historical group.[49] Now a radical difference remains, for the existence which takes its death into account as that which totalizes it is precisely, in so doing, prevented from truly opening itself to the future. There is a choice: If as the narrator of my own story I choose the Heideggerian anticipation, it is necessary to recognize that, regardless of whatever Heidegger says about it himself, the world is going to die with me. So, if I do not commit myself to the impossible project of salvaging my death as a fine end to my life, which is perhaps in fact going to be brutally interrupted, I can on the contrary engage myself in conceiving of some grand lines of a story to which my life belongs in spite of its finitude, and which goes beyond me as a particular individual.

The parallelism of which Carr speaks does not exist, i.e., that of knowing what is between the individual life in the Heideggerian sense and the collective life in the more Hegelian sense, the latter being constituted by the mutual recognition of participants in common projects. For no contribution to common works, whether it be the culture of the earth or the creation of art, shows "the death" of these works.

The grand narrative which transcends the individual biography not only towards the past but also towards the future has, however, a very considerable ethical importance; it is through it that all communality, small or large, thinks itself. This is also precisely the reason it is necessary to guard against all attempts to consider it as a **law** of the sort which comes to repress the members of the community or society whose narrative identity it constitutes.

What is called the post-modern critique of the Great Narrative finds its justification here. This critique takes up once again, on the occasion of the modern political experience of Stalinism and Nazism, etc., Kierkegaard's case against the Hegelians' Great Narrative of the history of the world. But the perversion of the historical narrative which assigns itself an authoritarian and absolutist role does not prove that all historical narrative ruins rather than edifies the good life. Considering that ethics reveals the relations between humans, it seems unreasonable to set aside only one life for the narrative, and refuse it a collective life as well, that is, refuse it the role of an ethical model calling everyone to make life better.

The question of knowing on what basis we judge narratives and distinguish between good and bad narrative testimonies has nevertheless been posed. One has called for human rights advocates to denounce the great narratives which justify injustice and the authoritarian state. But the same question can be asked with regard to these human rights: In the name of what are they judged valid?

Thus arises the question of knowing whether it is possible to formulate a fundamental principle of ethics.

THE QUEST FOR A FUNDAMENTAL PRINCIPLE OF ETHICS

Alan Donagan, in his **Theory of Morality** from 1977, treats what he calls "the fundamental principle of traditional ethics." For him, the great problem is not that of determining what the principle is, but of demonstrating its validity without reference to a religious conception. Thus he has been seeking to prove the validity of this principle on the basis of its "rationality," that is to say, on the basis of its ability to be applied in practical life without creating unacceptable conflicts and contradictions. The result of this demonstration would not only be a defense of a determinate principle, but moreover the general proof that a fundamental principle of ethics can be formulated and affirmed.

It is necessary, however, to ask what Donagan means by the "rationality" of the fundamental principle. He reproaches, in effect, the practical wisdom [phronesis] of Aristotle for being limited to life in the city-state, and not, like "the divine law" of the Stoics, to be "valid for all men in virtue of their common rationality."[50] In saying this he is not challenging the Aristotelian distinction between practical and theoretical rationality, but is rather affirming that that for which there is a practical reason should belong to man as such, and not be given to a privileged few, for example those who have the status of being male, adults and freemen of a city-state.

In Judaism and Christianity, Donagan rediscovers the idea that there is a moral law valid for the whole world; they have given us the conception of an ethical theory as "a theory of a system of laws or precepts, binding upon rational creatures as such, the content of which is ascertainable by human reason."[51]

In spite of the fact that many theologians, including Maimonides and Saint Thomas Aquinas, have believed that divine revelation is a better basis for ethics than reason alone, Donagan stresses[52] that the idea of an ethics founded on autonomous reason is maintained in the tradition; nevertheless it was for the first time made explicit by Kant in a serious and exemplary moral philosophy such as we find in the **Groundwork of the Metaphysic of Morals** of 1785.

The formula by which Kant defines the fundamental principle of this ethics is well known: "Act only on that maxim through which you can at the same time will that it should become a universal law."[53] One also knows the process that Hegel used in reproaching Kant for reducing ethics to an empty form thanks to subjectivity. He substituted there the idea of a *habitus* or, according to the expression dear to Donagan, of a **disposition of affection and guidance**, the content of which is conferred on him by the ethical community.

But Donagan insists that Kant's fundamental principle of ethics does not consist solely of the formal definition of the imperative, for Kant also gives a material definition: "Act in such a way that you always treat humanity, whether in your own person or in the person of any other, never simply as a means, but always at the same time as an end."[54] Now, according to Kant, these two formulae express the same moral law.

Donagan also notes that the Hegelian conception of ethics becomes embarrassed as soon as a person does not find, in his or her own society, norms meeting his or her notion of the ideal life. Hegel expresses this embarrassment himself in his **Principles of the Philosophy of Right**: "Since the world existing of freedom has become unfaithful to its ideal, the will no longer gains strength in its duties and cannot regain the harmony which actuality has lost, other than in the ideal world of the inner life."[55]

Donagan explains this dilemma by citing an historical narrative concerning an Austrian peasant, Franz Jägerstätter, who, despite the advice of his church and the order given by the state under Nazi domination, refused to serve as a soldier in the Hitlerian war he considered unjust--a courageous attitude he paid for with his life. In this case, Donagan says, it was the morality or the *Sittlichkeit* of the community which was empty, not the correct ethical conviction of the peasant.[56]

Thus, Donagan believes that instead of seeking the fundamental principle of ethics in social consensus, it would be better to examine the validity of the ethics which has been maintained as a guide to action for people of our culture for at least two thousand years. He performs this analysis in three stages: first he defines the first principle of this ethics. Then he attempts to show the consistency of the system of prescriptions which, according to him, follow from it in the form of "first-order precepts." His method here consists in dissolving the contradictions which one might be inclined to attribute to this system. A contradiction appears in effect if one and the same ethical system at the same time both permits (as conforming to reason) and prohibits (as contrary to the same reason) a determinate action. And third, he attempts to show that such contradictions disappear if one takes cases where a moral rule does not apply to be exceptions which can be justified by the very difficulties had in attempting to apply it. For example, Donagan maintains that it is permissible to break the rule: "One ought never lie without good reason," if the communication is not free, as in such cases as where one is speaking with children, the insane or those whose minds have been impaired by age or illness.[57]

In the same way Donagan undertakes—on the third level of his analysis—to make the contradictions between what he calls "second-order precepts" disappear, in order to be able to recognize those which appear when it is a question of the culpability or the non-culpability of the **intention** of the agent.

Now, we are not able here to enter into a discussion of all of the contradictions Donagan treats in order to affirm the validity of the traditional ethics, which remains for him principally "a system of laws or precepts about human actions considered objectively, as deeds."[58] Note, however, how he defines his fundamental precept. He does not find it in the formula expressing the Golden Rule (on which Ricoeur insists), since that rule, according to him, is inapplicable in the case where a unilateral action is demanded; for example, on the part of parents, teachers or judges with respect to children, students and those being judged. In addition, he says, the Golden Rule does not permit the judging of actions such as suicide, which concern no one but the agent, or actions which are consented to between two persons and have no effect upon a third. One can ask, it is true, whether this critique of the Golden Rule hits its target, but that would demand a whole discussion on the meaning of this rule, which I do not want to enter into here. We can leave this question unanswered insofar as what we are seeking is to clarify the way in which the fundamental principle of ethics is understandable, and not to decide what the principle precisely says.

Now Donagan finds the fundamental precept or principle in an interpretation of the rule expressed in **Lévitique**: "You shall love thy neighbour as thyself,"[59] and repeated by Jesus,[60] who interprets the "neighbour" as any human being whatever. Donagan finds the same "rational" interpretation in Kant's principles, which he summarizes thus: "It is impermissible not to respect every human being, oneself or any other, as a rational creature."[61]

In what follows, Donagan devotes himself to a consideration of permissible and non-permissible acts in order to establish a cogent "casuistic" system. On this point he also follows Kant who, in the **Groundwork** and later in his **Metaphysics of Morals** from 1797, insists that one must always, **without exception**, refrain from committing suicide, keep a promise, perfect one's natural gifts, help others in need, and so on.

But the establishment of a "casuistry" seems to me to be a very formidable enterprise which risks paralyzing action. This is evident as soon as one reflects upon current problems in medical ethics.[62] Two examples can suffice for us here. The first is that to keep a person alive using all available means shows the respect that one has for that person; but to relieve suffering by using medicines, although it shortens his or her life, is also to show respect. So, one must choose between two contradictory applications of the same moral rule.

The second example concerns the interdiction against lying; if we do not tell a dying man, for instance, the truth concerning his illness, we deceive him, and that is not to show him respect; but if we tell him his illness is terminal, we will perhaps discourage him in such a way that he passes the rest of his life in despair—not due to his illness, but because he no longer desires to live. How is one to establish a casuistry in these two domains? Is it not rather a question, in each situation, of taking into consideration the uniqueness of each person and his or her environment, and of subordinating all moral systematizing to the particular conditions involving the person in question?

I think, however, that the enterprise aimed at demonstrating the validity of a fundamental ethical principle by the coherence of a system of moral laws and prescriptions is condemned to failure, for one cannot deduce from situations where the principle is valid a coherent system which is always applicable to every case.

80

This is, moreover, why the implicit ethics of a poetic narrative always disappoint those who are looking for a strict morality, as John Dominique Crossan has said with regard to the "silence in the parables"; the deception derives from the fact that we obstinately seek "precepts and want programs."[63]

How does one then ensure the validity of a fundamental principle of ethics? If the application of a system of prescriptions deduced from the principle cannot show it to be pertinent to particular actions in all imaginable **situations**, then we are also obliged to abandon the idea that any particular **action** can be prescribed by the principle.

To be sure, we can without doubt establish rules which absolutely prohibit certain diabolical actions, as is the case regarding the prohibition of torture (the destruction of the human personality) and acts that would destroy the whole world and all humankind (via an atomic war or other universal crime). These actions are diabolical not only because they are destructive, but also because they are self-destructive; the torturer destroys his or her own personality in destroying that of the victim; and one who declares war against humanity surely declares war against him/herself as well. But absolute prohibitions in such cases concern only extreme acts and not a way of daily life. The prohibition of other acts (for example, lying, the breaking of promises, swindling and even homicide) can never be absolute, because one can always imagine exceptions (for example, killing an aggressor to prevent his or her killing a child, etc.).

It is true that moral laws impose themselves to protect human life against the destruction of one person by another or others. There is a moral law not only, as Ricoeur says (in keeping with the **Philosophie Morale** of Eric Weil), because there is violence, but because there is destruction, and above all self-destruction, which is the evil expressed in a pure form in such extreme acts as torture or war against humanity. Besides, a certain controlled violence, and not only that of the state, can be justifiable to protect human life against, for example, such fiends as take people hostage.

It is precisely because exceptions should be possible that moral laws are always subsumed under the fundamental principle of ethics, which can require their derogation or transformation. But this principle cannot itself be a moral law covering the performance or non-performance of particular kinds of daily actions.

The mistake made by all the moralists is to try to apply the fundamental principle of ethics to particular acts instead of applying them to **ethical attitudes**. Roger Mehl has devoted an admirable little book to this point in which he declares that such attitudes are to be found "in the background of my acts"[64] and constitute "a certain fidelity amongst themselves."[65] They are "a sort of **structuring** of my existence" and they "help us to justify our acts."[66]

So we find once again at the basis of ethics the *habitus* or *hexis* in the Aristotelian sense, the path or way of life according to practical wisdom. Thus we can say that the great commandment: **Love thy neighbor**, and its Christian transformation into the expression of unlimited generosity: **Love your enemies**,[67] express the affirmation of the **principle of a fundamental attitude**. And it is the same thing when one defines the Golden Rule. This rule only makes sense as a principle of an attitude which holds for all possible relations between human beings.

The prescriptions of attitudes are situated on the level of ethical intention of which Ricoeur speaks. They concern the paths by which one **pursues** a happy life with others, negatively by protecting one's liberty, health, security, and so on, and positively by realizing a true sense of community. They are fundamental because they are always capable of giving valid responses to the question: What should I do to live the good life?

Kant's error is not to be found in the **expression** of the categorical imperative: "Act only on that maxim through which you can at the same time will that it should become a universal law,"[68] for it could well serve as the maxim of a fundamental **attitude**. But his error consists in applying his principle not to ethical attitudes but to specific good deeds (since he speaks of refusing to commit suicide, keeping a promise, telling the truth, and so on). From whence does his moralist rigorism come, which does not limit itself to requiring good will but demands the observation without exception of certain prescriptions or "duties"? When we transgress a duty, he declares, we "take the liberty of making an **exception** to [the maxim expressing the duty] for ourselves,"[69] as though the maxim were, in his own terms, "a universal law of nature."[70] For Kant there is nothing between good will and concrete action. His weakness lies in his not having seen that the ethical attitude inserts itself between the two, and so mediates the realization of the will in action.

Nevertheless, Kant's material principle admirably provides us with the expression of the fundamental ethical attitude so well suited to our technological age: "Act in such a way that you always treat humanity, whether in your own person or in the person of any other, never simply as a means, but always at the same time as an end"—never simply as a computer, for example. Here what we see is clearly not a rule for a particular action, but a principle for a way of living, for an attitude which is valid for any imaginable action.

Unfortunately, Kant could not completely resist the temptation of presenting this practical imperative as a rational algorithm when he said that if the whole world performed certain acts (broke promises, for example), society would be impossible. He maintained, in effect, that in a world where it was permitted to break promises or to lie, "it would be futile to profess a will for future action to others who would not believe my profession or who, if they did so over-hastily, would pay me back in like coin."[72] And this is also a problem for the Golden Rule, for it too can be understood as a calculus.

This calculus certainly has its validity as a **utilitarian** principle on the social level, but ethics cannot be reduced to what is socially reasonable, expressing a compromise in the struggle between different interests. In that case there would be nothing other than reciprocal egoism. To be valid as an expression of human dignity, ethics must be such an expression also in social situations where reciprocity of interests is excluded or very little practicable, where it is a question of reciprocal generosity.

Thus the universal ethics, which underlies true fellowship, should be based on the narrative tradition which testifies to the attitude of generosity. This attitude, according to Mehl, "consists in giving credit to others, at least in crediting them with good faith, and for this reason affording them what they ask for or even what they do not ask for, that to which they are not entitled." However, there is only generosity, he says, "when in my relations with others, I do not hold myself to the rules of strict equity, but add a sort of surplus to what is due."[73]

We add in conclusion that this generosity acquired through our narrative experience of daily life becomes a fundamental attitude which is recognized and venerated thanks solely to the poetic narratives which affirm the high value of recounting the fictive or historical scenes of the good life. These scenes become as a consequence privileged by our philosophical reflection on the basis of ethics. They make the basis of our ethics, like narratives and imaginary models of their fundamental principle, models which provide us with the possibility of evaluating all other narratives and judging all actions and rules of action.

University of Copenhagen

83   Translated by Craig Dilworth

ENDNOTES

1. Cf. my "Éthique et narrativité," to appear in English in the volume devoted to Ricoeur in the series **Living Philosophers**, and published in French in a shorter form in **Aquinas** (1986), pp. 211-232.

2. **Res Publica**, No. 9, Symposion, Lund, 1987, p. 125.

3. *Idem.*

4. In the **Encyclopédia Universalis**, Symposium, Paris, 1985, pp. 42-45.

5. From 1979; reprinted in **Du Texte à l'action**, Seuil, 1986, pp. 237-259.

6. **Encyclopédia Universalis**, p. 42, 1; cf. Ricoeur's "The Problem of the Foundation of Moral Philosophy," **Philosophy Today** (Fall, 1978), p. 176.

7. *Ibid.,* p. 42, 2; cf. "The Problem ...," p. 178.

8. *Ibid.,* p. 43, 1.

9. *Idem.*

10. *Idem.*; cf. "The Problem...," pp. 178-179.

11. *Idem.*; cf. "The Problem ...," p. 179.

12. *Ibid.,* p. 43, 2.

13. *Ibid.,* p. 45, 1.

14. *Idem.*

15. **Du texte à l'action**, Seuil, 1986, p. 247.

16. *Ibid.,* p. 249.

17. *Idem.*

18. *Idem.*

19. *Ibid.,* p. 250.

20. Paul Ricoeur, **Time and Narrative**, Chicago: University of Chicago Press, Vol. I, 1984, p. 55.

21. *Ibid.,* pp. 56-57.

22. Aristotle, **Poetics**, 1454b 8-9.

23. *Ibid.,* 1448a 16-17.

24. James M. Redfield, **Nature and Culture in the Iliad**, Chicago: University of Chicago Press, 1975.

25. **Time and Narrative**, Vol. I, p. 59.

26. *Ibid.,* Vol. I, p. 113.

27. "Éthique et Narrativité," **Aquinas**, 1986, p. 218.

28. **Time and Narrative**, Vol. I, p. 113.

29. *Ibid.,* Vol. I, p. 115.

30. David Carr, **Time, Narrative and History**, Bloomington: Indiana University Press, p. 19.

31. *Ibid.,* p. 51.

32. *Ibid.,* p. 61.

33. Alasdair MacIntyre, **After Virtue**, Notre Dame: University of Notre Dame Press, 1981, p. 197.

34. Carr, p. 71.

35. *Ibid.,* p. 74.

36. Wilhelm Schapp, **In Geschichten verstrickt**, Wiesbaden: B. Heymann, 1976, p. 103.

37. *Ibid.,* p. 96.

38. Jean-Paul Sartre, **Cahiers pour une morale**, Paris: Gallimard, 1983, p. 292.

39. *Idem.*

40. *Ibid.,* p. 299.

41. Aristotle, **Nichomachean Ethics**, 1098b 18-19.

42. MacIntyre, p. 189.

43. *Ibid.,* p. 191.

44. *Ibid.,* p. 194.

45. *Ibid.,* p. 205.

46. *Ibid.*, p. 174ff.

47. Dominique Crossan, **In Parables**, New York: Harper and Row, 1973, p. 33.

48. *Ibid.*, pp. 80-81.

49. Carr, p. 164.

50. Alan Donagan, **The Theory of Morality**, Chicago: University of Chicago Press, 1977, p. 4.

51. *Ibid.*, p. 7.

52. *Ibid.*, pp. 8-9.

53. Immanuel Kant, **Groundwork of the Metaphysic of Morals**, original edition, p. 421.

54. *Ibid.*, p. 429.

55. Sec. 138; referred to by Donagan, p. 14.

56. *Ibid.*, pp. 15-17.

57. *Ibid.*, p. 89.

58. *Ibid.*, p. 52.

59. **Lévitique**, pp. 18-19.

60. Luke, 10: 25-28.

61. Donagan, p. 66.

62. Cf. my **Éthique et médecine**, Paris: Tierce et INSERM, 1987, p. 10.

63. Crossan, p. 82.

64. Roger Mehl, **Les attitudes morales**, Paris: P.U.F., 1971, p. 6.

65. *Ibid.*, p. 7.

66. *Ibid.*, p. 10.

67. Mathew, 5: 43-44.

68. Kant, **Groundwork**, p. 421.

69. *Ibid.*, p. 424; it is Kant who emphasizes the word "exception."

70. *Ibid.*, p. 421.

71. *Ibid.,* p. 429.

72. *Ibid.,* p. 403.

73. Roger Mehl, **Les attitudes morales**, p. 96.

paul ricoeur
the human being as
the subject matter
of philosophy*

In this paper, I pose the following question: "What kind of discourse may philosophers use about humans[1] that scientists, as such, are not equipped to use?"

This way of characterizing philosophy by its discourse does not merely reflect the linguistic turn that most contemporary philosophies have taken; it displays the affinity that philosophy enjoys with its subject-matter itself, to the extent that the least disputable feature of our humanity is the use of language articulated as discourse. In this way, the philosophical discourse arises within the space of reflexivity opened up by the various discourses that we use about the world, ourselves and other people. But this mediation provided by the reflexivity of discourse in general between philosophy and its topic, when this topic is the human being, does not imply that philosophical discourse should proceed in a direct, immediate, and intuitive way from this spontaneous reflexivity. With Kant, I assume that the question: **What is a human?**, far from constituting the first question that philosophy is able to raise, comes at the end of a series of prior questions such as: **What can I know? What must I do? What am I allowed to hope?** I do not claim that these three Kantian questions are the only ones that can introduce the decisive question: What is a human? My only claim is that, in order not to remain trivial, the answer to this question must appear as the

paul ricoeur ultimate outcome of a series of preparatory steps. The itinerary which I invite you to follow is not indeed a reply to the one delineated by the famous Kantian motto. It nevertheless is derived from it as regards a decisive trait, i.e., the implication of the personal pronoun "I" in each of the three questions quoted above. It is the direct and progressive construction of the meaning of the term "I" that I attempt by taking jointly into account the resources of analytical philosophy, phenomenology, and hermeneutics, to quote only the philosophical disciplines with which I am the most closely associated.

The successive stages of our itinerary will proceed from a more abstract toward a more concrete characterization of the kind of being that we assume to be by contradistinction with things and animals. By convention we shall call **persons**, in the most natural sense, this kind of being, and will work through progressive characterization by which persons deserve to be called selves. From "persons" to "selves," such could be the title of my paper. It is useless to insist that the order of my presentation has no historical bearing and rules only the progression from one level of discourse to another.

Linguistic Level

The first stage is that of **linguistic** analysis, in the philosophical sense of the term linguistic. It has to do with the universal—or the most universal—features of our language when we speak meaningfully about humans as persons and selves. For that purpose, I will rely, in turn, on **semantics** in the sense of Frege, and on **pragmatics** in the sense of Morris.

At the level of **semantics**, persons cannot be characterized as selves to the extent that, in the Fregean sense, semantics has only to do with propositions according to the rules of an extensional logic for which the attitudes of the speaker and, more generally, the circumstances of interlocution, are irrelevant. Nevertheless, in spite of the narrowness of these limitations, something can be said about humans as persons within the framework of a philosophical semantics.

How do we do that?

1. Two universal properties of language have to be considered. On the one hand, language is structured in such a way that it may designate **individuals**, thanks to specific operators of individualization such as definite descriptions, proper names and deictics, including the demonstrative adjectives and pronouns, the personal pronouns, and the verbal tenses. Of course, all the individuals pointed to by way of these operators are not persons.

90

Persons are individuals of a certain kind; but it is to the singularity of persons that we are peculiarly interested for reasons which will appear later and which are specifically connected with the status of persons as selves, i.e., as self-individuating. Thanks to the individualizing intent of these operators, we may designate one and only one person and may distinguish it from all the others; that is part of what we call identification. To identify persons as individuals constitutes the most elementary and abstract step of a philosophical discourse about humans.

To this first property of language we must add a more specific constraint which still belongs to the level of a semantics considered from the point of view of its **referential** implications. According to this constraint, to which Peter Strawson's classical work, **Individuals**, is devoted, we are unable to identify a given particular without classifying it either as **body** or as **person**. I do not discuss here the arguments which compel us to say, first, that bodies and persons are the basic particulars to which we may refer by speaking as we do about the components of the world, and second, that these two classes are the only legitimate basic particulars. I take these arguments for granted for the sake of our further analysis and want rather to focus on the three constraints that are linked to the status of persons as basic particulars. First, persons have to be bodies in order to be persons; second, the psychical predicates that distinguish persons from bodies have to be attributed to the same entity as the predicates common to persons and bodies, let us say physical predicates; third, psychical predicates are such that they hold the same meaning when applied to oneself or to someone else—or, to put it as Strawson does, whether self-ascribable or other-ascribable.

As we may observe, persons are not already selves at this level of discourse, to the extent that they are not dealt with as **self-designative** entities; they are some of the things **about which** we speak, i.e., **referred-to** entities. Nevertheless, this achievement of language should not be underestimated, to the extent that by referring to persons as basic particulars we begin to assign a logical status to the third grammatical person "he" and "she", even if only in the pragmatical approach, the third person is more than a grammatical person, i.e., a person as a self. This full right of the third person in our discourse about persons is confirmed by the place that literature assigns to the protagonists of most narrative, mainly in **Er-Erzählung**, to use a category familiar to German narratology.

That a philosophical discourse about humans cannot be confined within the boundaries of identifying reference in an extensional logic is already suggested by each of the three features of the person corresponding to the logical constraints proper to the characterization of the person as a basic particular. First, the body that the person is "also" is not only a body among all other bodies, but my body, my own body; the possession pointed to by the deictic "my"/"mine" seems to imply a subject able to designate himself/herself as the one who **has** this body. Second, the joint attribution of physical and psychical predicates to the **same** entity, i.e., the person, seems to exceed the features of attribution in the logical sense of mere predication to a logical subject. This odd kind of attribution deserves to be called **ascription** in order to take into account its relation to ownership and its kinship with the moral imputation that we will consider later. Third, the kind of sameness that psychical predicates keep, whether self- or other-ascribable, already alludes to the **distinction** between self and other: this cannot be done within the framework of logical semantics.

2. A second stage in the philosophical discourse about humans is represented by the transition from semantics to pragmatics, i.e., to a situation in which the meaning of a proposition is dependent on the context of interlocution. It is at that stage that the "I" and the "you" implied in the process of interlocution can be thematized for the first time. The best way to illustrate this is to assume the framework of the theory of speech-acts and to rely on the **distinction** between locutionary and illocutionary acts. The illocutionary force of such utterances as stating, promising, warning, etc., can easily be made explicit by emphasizing the intentional prefixes including the term "I" which bring to the level of expression this illocutionary force. Speech-acts may be in this way rewritten as I state, I promise, I warn, etc. The step forward in the characterization of the person as self is obvious: whereas at the level of semantics the person was only one of the things about which we speak, at the level of pragmatics the person is immediately designated as self, to the extent that in the intentional prefix, both the speaker and the addressee are implied as **self-designating**. But it is not only the "I" and the "you" that are brought to the forefront by this process of self-designation. The structure of language is such that we may ascribe to a third person—the person about whom we speak—the same ability to designate himself/herself as the one who speaks and to designate his/her addressee. Quotation is the ordinary way of securing this transfer; "he thinks," "she thinks" means: such-and-such person says in his or her heart: "I think that," with quotation marks; in narratives, this assignment of self-designating acts to the protagonists of the story is usual; in plays, the quotation marks are lifted by the scenic situation, and the dialogue between the actors who embody the characters is directly shown. Strictly speaking, the third person—in the grammatical sense—is not fully a person beside this transfer of the self-designation of the one who speaks and says "I" to the person about whom we are speaking. Thanks to this

transfer, the pragmatics of the "I-You" is grafted onto the semantics of the "He/She."

This remarkable achievement of pragmatics does not prevent the act of self-designation from being loaded with paradoxes. The first one is still easy to solve. It proceeds from the ambiguity of the expression "I." As a member of the paradigm of personal pronouns, the term "I" is an empty or vacant term, able to designate anyone who, by using it, designates him/herself; but, when actually uttered by someone, the term "I" designates one and only one person, the one who uses it. In the first case, "I" is a **shifter** in relation to which a number of virtual utterers may be substituted for one another; in the second case, "I" designates a unique unsubstitutable perspective on the world.[2]

A second, more intractable, paradox arises from the attempt to ascribe an epistemological status to the "I" in use, therefore to the "I" as designating **my** unsubstitutable perspective on the world. To the extent that the **ego** of an actual utterance does not belong to the content of any of its statements, then we have to say with Wittgenstein that the **ego** as a singular perspectival center is the limit of the world and **none** of its contents. To put this paradox in other words, the utterance as an act may be held as an event which occurs in the world as my walking or eating, whereas the speaking self—the utterance's utterer—is not an event; he/she cannot be said to occur.

This paradox is not at all an artifact of philosophical analysis. It is reflected in ordinary language by the ways we introduce ourselves to someone else as being Mr. or Ms. so-and-so. This is what we call identifying oneself. Now, identification taken in this sense of self-identification relies on the adjunction to the unsubstitutable **ego** of a name borrowed from the public list of possible proper names according to specific rules and conventions proper to a given culture. The aporia of Wittgenstein's **Tractatus** reappears in a new form, as we read in the **Blue Book**: how do we connect the "I" limit of the world with a proper name which designates a real individual belonging to this world? How can I say: "I, Paul Ricoeur?"

In order to solve this aporia, we must find some specific procedures capable of securing interaction between the semantical characterization of a given person as **this** or **that** person and the pragmatical characterization of the self as "I" and "you." We find a model for securing this interaction in the way we connect, by means of the calendar, the absolute **now** of the living present with a certain **date**, i.e., a position in the system of all possible dates established by the institution of the calendar. It is in the same way that we connect the absolute **here** determined by the position of my own body with a **place** in geometrical space; we achieve this connection by the procedures of localization with the help of maps which play a role parallel to that of the calendar. Following the model of datation and localization corresponding to the deictics "now" and "here," we connect the absolute "I" and its unsubstitutable perspective on the world with the person, at which point the identifying reference; thanks to a procedure similar to that of datation with the help of the calendar and to that of localization with the help of maps this procedure is that of **naming**; it relies on some social convention that amounts to an **inscription** of the "I" on the social map of family names and personal names. Thanks to this **inscription**, a self-referring **ego** is said to be the same as one of the persons now existing in the world. Self-identification is nothing else than this correlation between self-designation and referential identification.

At the end of the first part of our journey, a question may be raised concerning the relationship between analytic philosophy and phenomenology. Are we able to make sense of these procedures of datation, localization, and name assignments without trespassing the boundaries of linguistic analysis? Are we not compelled to inquire about the kind of being which allows this twofold way of identification as objective person and self-designating subject? The very notion of a singular perspective has unavoidable ontological connotations. What is this singular perspectival position if not that of my own body? Now embodiment, i.e., the very fact that I am **this** body, i.e., a something in the world, is not an isolated phenomenon. It is part of a broader ontological structure; I mean my **belonging-to** what Husserl called *Lebenswelt* and Heidegger *In-der-Welt-sein*. And we have here a certain preunderstanding of what it means to belong in a corporeal way to the world. This preunderstanding was already implied in the paradoxes of the **ascription** of predicates to this special entity that we call a person. What we understand in this preunderstanding is the primitive fact that my body as a body among other bodies is a mere fragment of the objective experience of the world, and that my body as mine shares the status of the **ego** as the limit reference-point of the world.

To my mind, this convergence between linguistic analysis and phenomenology must be understood as a reciprocal implication; the ontology of embodiment would remain an inconsistent claim if it were not articulated in a semantics and a pragmatics in such a way that the double allegiance of my own body to the world of events and to that of the self could be reflected in the procedures of language which connect the person as something about which we do speak and the self implied in the reflective properties of speech acts.

Practical Level

In the second part of my presentation, I want to make more concrete our characterization of the person as a self by connecting the notion of **speaking** subject to that of **acting** subject. In a sense, this characterization occurs at the crossing-point between semantics and pragmatics to the extent that an important feature of human action as rule-governed behavior is ruled by language and, more specifically, by most speech-acts. In other words, human action is **spoken** action. On the one hand, we speak about actions as events happening in the world: in this sense, the theory of action is a province of semantics; we speak actually of the semantics of action. On the other hand, we designate ourselves as the agents of our actions. The theory of action, then, appears as a province of pragmatics. But the topic of action is so specific that the theory of action has become nowadays a discipline of its own.

Let us **check** the autonomy of the theory of action in the borderline of both semantics and pragmatics.

In the terms of logical semantics, actions are events of a unique kind. Indeed, an event may be called an action to the extent that it is, or has been, done intentionally, or with the intention of doing something else, or as the fulfillment of a previous intention, which in turn may be postponed, suspended, or even cancelled. In this last case, intention is pure intention, aiming at an action to be done by one whose fulfillment is contingent upon inner or outer circumstances.

The characterization of actions as intentional in one of the three uses of the term intention (intentionally, with the intention of, pure intention) raises numerous problems on the borderline of semantics. The main discussion has focused on the question of whether intentions should be interpreted as **reasons for**, and in this case held irreducible to **causes** in the Humean sense, or whether intentions, even described as reasons-for, should be explained in terms of causes. The difficulty is the following: If desires and beliefs are equated with propositional attitudes in order to comply with the requirements of extensional logic, a logical gap appears between the semantics of our propositions about actions and the everyday experience of being able to do something and of doing it, i.e., of **making** events happen. The difficulty may remain hidden as long as we treat intentions as features of action already done, therefore, in the adverbial form quoted above: something done intentionally. Intention may be held as a modification of action as event occurring in the world.

95   The difficulty becomes somewhat explicit when we speak of the

intention with which we do something. But this difficulty appears intractible when we consider intentions not yet fulfilled or even unfulfilled, i.e., "pure" intentions. Then intentions have to be dealt with as a species of the genus "intentionality," as the paradigm of anticipation and self-projection. Both features—temporality and personal commitment—require once more the mutual help of logical semantics and of phenomenology. Within the mixed discipline proceeding from this interaction, phenomenology provides the general category of intentionality, with its two sides, *noesis* and *noema*; and semantics articulates the noematic side of intentionality in the terms of its analysis of sentences of action.

A similar connection between phenomenology and analytic philosophy arises on the borderline of pragmatics. Here the focus of discussion is no longer the relation between motives as reasons-for and causes as events occurring in the world but the very relation between action and agent. It is no longer the link between the **what?** and the **why?** of action, as on the level of semantics, but between the **who?** and the **what-and-why?** of action. The question of the **who?** of action raises in a new way the question of the **ascription** of psychical and physical predicates to the person considered as the subject of predication.

This question is no less puzzling for analytic philosophy than for phenomenology. It is a fact that in the field of the philosophy of action the care devoted to the clarification of the relations between the **what?** and the **why?** of action has obscured, if not made irrelevant, the relation between the **who?** and the **what-and-why?** This is peculiarly striking in D. Davidson's treatment of the problem of action; the identification of reasons-for with causes leads to a drastic reduction of actions to kinds of events. The category of events, as happening out there, displays no affinity with the category of selfhood and tends rather to exclude it. But this exclusion betrays a specific trait of action, namely, the fact that it is a part of the meaning of intention that it makes action **depend on us as agents**.

Ordinary language confirms this assumption: the agency of the agent is usually expressed with the help of such metaphors as parenthood, mastery, or ownership (the last being incorporated into the grammar of the so-called possessive adjectives and pronouns). These linguistic facts call for a new articulation of our philosophical discourse about selfhood. Husserl raised the problem in terms of an egology where the **ego** is called the "intentional pole" of the numerous and variable acts proceeding from it, or as the luminous source of as many rays of light. But *Ichpol* and *Ichstrahle* are only other metaphors. How, then, to give a conceptual articulation to this intuitive grasp?

96

New aporias appear at this point: How to give an account of the double status of psychical predicates as, on the one hand, keeping the same meaning whether self- or other-ascribable, therefore as floating entities indifferent to actual ascriptions, and, on the other hand, as actually ascribed to someone who **owns** them? Another aporia: What kind of relation is there between ascription and moral imputation? Does one ascribe to someone in the same way a judge rules that something belongs legally to somebody? But does not legal and moral imputation presuppose the confidence that an agent has that he or she is the author of his or her acts? And do not this confidence and this assurance—when conceptualized—bring us back to the third cosmological antinomy of Kant's **Dialectic of Pure Reason**, which opposes the **Thesis** according to which we are able to **initiate** actual beginnings in the course of the world and the **Antithesis** which requires an infinite *regressus* in the open series of causes?

As concerns the mixed models, such as Von Wright's in **Explanation and Understanding**, they rightly require a tight connection between practical syllogisms and systemic concatenations in order to make sense of the familiar notion of **initiative** as the intentional intervention of self-reflecting agents in the course of events. But this very connection between teleological and causal segments of action seems to call once more for another kind of discourse than that of analytical philosophy. A phenomenology of the "I can," following Merleau-Ponty, seems to be required in order to make sense of the belonging of the agent to the world considered itself as a practical field, with paths and obstacles. Is not the preunderstanding of our own belonging to the world as a practical field previous to the distinction between a semantics of action as events and a pragmatics of self-designating agents? Once more, what makes the phenomenology of the "I can" more fundamental than linguistic analysis, whether semantical or pragmatical, is its close affinity with an ontology of the **proper** body, i.e., of a body which is also **my** body and which, thanks to this twofold allegiance, constitutes the connecting link between an **agency** which is **ours** and a system of events which occurs in the world. Once more, too, I agree that the phenomenology of the "I can" and the pertaining ontology of the proper body and of the world as practical field cannot be discursively articulated without the help of a semantics and a pragmatics of our discourse related to actions and agents, even at the price of the aporias which puzzled Kant, Schopenhauer, Wittgenstein, and Merleau-Ponty.

Ethical Level

In the third and last part of my paper, I show how the moral dimension of **imputation** may be grafted onto the previous characterizations of persons as selves. **Moral imputation** consists in a kind of judgment, saying that humans are **responsible** for the proximate consequences of their deeds and for that reason may be praised or blamed.[3] Such a judgment relies on the previous descriptions of the agent as the owner and author of his or her action and, beyond this, on the identification of the person as a basic particular and of the self as implied in the self-designation of the speaking subject. In this sense, both the linguistic and the practical aspects of selfhood are presupposed by the notion of moral imputation and responsibility. But new components are brought forth by this notion. Some are mere expansions of the previous category of action, some require a specific treatment.

As an expansion of the previous category of action, I want to introduce three features whose ethical bearing is at least implicit. We have first to consider the hierarchical structure of such complex actions as those which deserve to be called **practices**: technical skills, jobs, arts, games, etc. Compared to simple gestures, practices consist in chains of action displaying relations of coordination and, above all, of subordination; thanks to the structure of "embedment" proceeding from the latter, practices may in turn be included in **plans of life**, ordering professional life, family life, leisure, social, and political activities.

To this "logical" structure of practices and plans of life we add the "historical" character that practices and plans of life owe to their belonging to the unity of a life unfolding from birth to death. We may call this **second** trait of complex actions historical, not only because the unfolding of a unique life has temporal dimension, but also because this temporality is brought to language in a **narrative** form; in this sense, we may speak of the narrative unity of a life. Narrativity constitutes in this way an immanent structure of action. As H. Arendt has it, it is in stories that the "who of action" can be said, i.e., has to be told. Historical narratives, in the sense of historiography and fictional narratives, are grafted onto this immanent narrativity which equates a human life with one or many "life-stories."

A third feature of action has to be underscored, which may still be considered as an expansion of our previous analysis: its **teleological** structure, namely, the connection between means and ends already points toward this trait. Still more, the reference of practices and plans of life to the horizon of a "good life" as it is projected by individuals and communities. The new conceptual components that we now take into account are grafted onto this logical, historical, and teleological structure of action, which allows us to speak of human actions in terms of **praxis**.

The first ethical component is continuous with the teleological structure of complex action; this is why the ethical doctrines which emphasize it deserve themselves to be called teleological. Nevertheless, a new factor has to be introduced here, that of **value** and **evaluation**. It is to the extent that practices and plans of life are ruled by **precepts**—technical, aesthetic, moral, political—that actions can be evaluated, i.e., hierarchically ordered according to their relative compliance with these precepts. As long as the precepts ruling this evaluative process remain immanent to the practice itself, we may call them, with A. MacIntyre, **standards of excellence**, measuring the degree of achievement or of failure of a given activity. Standards of excellence define the good immanent to practice in such a way that the practice called medical characterizes immediately the physician as a "good" physician. It is the task of moral philosophy, then, to elaborate an explicit typology of the values implied to these standards of excellence. This is done in an ethics of virtues.

It is not my task here even to sketch such a typology of values, still less to construe hastily an ethics of virtues. The only task relevant to the purpose of my paper is to show the potential contribution of such processes of **evaluation** to the constitution of the person as self. I suggest that by evaluating our actions, we contribute in a specific way to the interpretation of our own selves in ethical terms. As Charles Taylor has it in his **Philosophical Papers**, "Man [woman] is a self-interpreting animal." But this self-interpretation is neither simple nor direct; it takes the roundabout way of the ethical assessment of our actions. The enlargement of our concept of selfhood resulting from this indirect process of evaluation applied to action is tremendous. The self—i.e., the "**who** of action"—does not merely consist in the self-designation of humans as the owners and the authors of their deeds; it implies also the self-interpretation in terms of the achievements and failures of what we called practices and plans of life. I suggest that we call **self-esteem** the interpretation of ourselves mediated by the ethical evaluation of our actions. Self-esteem is itself an evaluation process indirectly applied to ourselves as selves.

The second ethical component of moral imputation calls for a consideration which has been completely overlooked in all our previous analysis. I mean the **conflictual** structure of action as interaction. That all action is interaction could have been derived from our previous analysis of action as practice and *praxis*. But the important fact is not that action has a dialogical structure but that a specific kind of asymmetry seems to be linked to any transaction. The phenomenon which deserves to be underscored here is the fact that, by acting, someone exerts a power over somebody else; thus interaction does not merely confront agents equally capable of initiative but agents and patients as well: it's this asymmetry within action as interaction between agents and patients which gives way to the most decisive ethical considerations. Not that power as such implies violence; I say only that the power exerted by someone on somebody else constitutes the basic occasion for using the other as an instrument, which is the beginning of violence, murder, and still more torture, this being the extreme.

My claim, then, is that it is violence and the process of **victimization** generated by violence which invite us to add a deontological dimension to the teleological dimension of ethics. The latter gives way to an ethics of virtues, the former to an ethics of obligation which I see summarized in the second formulation of the categorical imperative: "Treat humanity in your own person and in the person of the other not only as a means but also as an end in itself." I insist that it is not desire but violence that compels us to give to morality the character of obligation, either in the negative form of prohibition—"You shall not kill"—or in the positive form of commandment—"You shall treat the patient of your action as an agent like yourself" (Gewirth).

Once more, I confess that this is not the place for a complete justification of the concept of obligation. We must leave unanalyzed the complex relationships between a teleological and a deontological foundation of morality. What is, rather, relevant to our topic is to disentangle and make explicit the new feature of selfhood corresponding to the deontological stage of morality. If **self-esteem** was the subjective correlative to the ethical evaluation of actions, then **respect** is the subjective correlative of moral obligation. But whereas self-esteem might imply only me, me alone, respect is directly structured as a dialogical category in the same way that interaction implied conflict; there is no self-respect without respect for the other. We should even have to say that if I esteem myself, I respect myself as someone else, as another. It is the other in myself that I respect. Conscience is the witness of this internalization of otherness in self-respect. Notice that respect does not abolish self-esteem but includes it; this may be the key to a correct interpretation of the strange commandment to love my neighbor as myself; this commandment interprets self-esteem and respect for the other in terms of one another.

At the end of this too quick a journey, I make two final remarks: First, the successive stages of our inquiry should not be dealt with in a serial way but in a cumulative way; the ethical dimensions are grafted onto the practical ones in the same way as the practical ones are grafted onto the linguistic dimensions. We must be capable of describing persons as basic particulars and selves as self-designating subjects of discourse in order to be able to characterize actions as intentionally-brought-forth events, and agents as the owners and authors of their actions; and we must

the human being as the subject matter of philosophy

understand what agency means in order to apply to actions a moral judgment of imputation and to call persons responsible selves. Such is the inner connectedness of the system of presuppositions which structures one of the possible philosophical discourses about human beings.

Second, the elaboration of this system of presuppositions should be assigned to philosophy, not to science, to the extent that it has to do with the conditions of the possibility of any empirical science concerning humans, not with facts pertaining to these sciences. Such notions as basic particulars, self-reference, agency, imputation, and responsibility may be held as transcendental conditions of the so-called human sciences. Philosophy, in this sense, is a long footnote at the bottom of this declaration, uttered with fear and trembling: *"Nous voici, nous les humains, nous les mortels!"*

Université de Paris

ENDNOTES

* This paper was presented at the World Congress of Philosophy, Brighton, August 1988.

1. I shall use the inclusive language "humans" instead of "men," which is suspect to many of us.

2. Husserl puts the expression "I" among the necessary occasional meanings; his analysis is not far from Russell's theory of "egocentric particulars." This ambiguity may be prevented by distinguishing with Peirce between I as a "type" and I as a "token." But we must add that the type is such that it must be assigned to someone and that in an exclusive way.

3. Imputation and responsibility are synonyms, the only difference being that it is actions which are **imputed** to someone and it is persons that are held **responsible** for actions and their consequences.

frans vansina
selected bibliography of ricoeur's english works

This bibliographical article is a revised and updated version of the list of Ricoeur's English writings published in: **Paul Ricoeur. A Primary and Secondary Systematic Bibliography (1935-1984)**. Leuven: Peeters, 1985, 8-15, 92-111.

Books

1965

History and Truth (Northwestern University Studies in Phenomenology and Existential Philosophy). Translation of several articles with an introduction by Ch. A. KELBLEY. Evanston (Illinois): Northwestern University Press, 1965, 24 x 15,5, xxxiv-333 p. Reprints in 1973, 1977 and 1979.

Fallible Man. Translation of **L'homme fallible** with an introduction by Ch. A. KELBLEY. [Chicago: Henry Regnery], [1965], 21 x 14,5 [bound], 17 x 10,5, xxix-224 p. [paper, Gateway Editions].

1966

Freedom and Nature: The Voluntary and the Involuntary (Northwestern University Studies in Phenomenology and

Existential Philosophy). Translation of **Le volontaire et l'involontaire** with an introduction by E.V. KOHAK. Evanston (Illinois): Northwestern University Press, 1966, 23,5 x 16,5, xl-498 p. [hardbound and paperbound]. Reprints in 1970, 1979 and 1984.

1967

Husserl. An Analysis of His Phenomenology (Northwestern University Studies in Phenomenology and Existential Philosophy). Translation of several articles with an introduction by E.G. BALLARD and L.E. EMBREE. Evanston (Illinois): Northwestern University Press, 1967, 23,5 x 16,5, xxii-238 p. [hardbound and paperbound]. Reprints in 1970, 1979 and 1984.

The Symbolism of Evil (Religious Perspectives, 17). Translation of **La symbolique du mal** by E. BUCHANAN. New York-Evanston-London: Harper and Row, [1967], 21 x 14,5, xv-357 p. [bound]; Boston: Beacon Press, 1969, 13,5 x 10,5, 362 p. [Beacon Paperbacks, 323]. Reprint of paperback edition in 1970.

1970

Freud and Philosophy: An Essay on Interpretation. Translation of **De l'interprétation. Essai sur Freud** by D. SAVAGE. New Haven and London: Yale University Press, 1970, 24 x 16 [bound], 1977 [paper], x-573 p.

1973

RICOEUR P. and MARCEL G., **Tragic Wisdom and Beyond** including **Conversations between Paul Ricoeur and Gabriel Marcel** (Northwestern University Studies in Phenomenology and Existential Philosophy). Translations of **Pour une sagesse tragique** by G. MARCEL and of **Entretiens Paul Ricoeur-Gabriel Marcel** with a preface and an introduction by P. McCORMICK and St. JOLIN. Evanston (Illinois): Northwestern University Press, 1973, 23,5 x 15,5 xxxv-256 p.

1974

The Conflict of Interpretations. Essays in Hermeneutics (Northwestern University Studies in Phenomenology and Existential Philosophy). Translation of **Le conflit des interprétations. Essais d'hermeneutique** by several authors with an introduction by the editor D. IHDE. Evanston (Illinois): Northwestern University Press, 1974, 23,5 x 16, xxv-512 p. [hardbound and paperbound]. Reprints in 1979, 1981 and 1984.

bibliography Political and Social Essays. Translation of several essays with a preface by P. RICOEUR and an introduction by the editors D. STEWART and J. BIEN. Athens: Ohio University Press, [1974], 22,5 x 14,5, ix-293 p.

1976

Interpretation Theory: Discourse and the Surplus of Meaning. Preface by T. KLEIN, Fort Worth (Texas): The Texas Christian University Press, [1976], 22,5 x 15, xii-107 p. Reprint in 1978.

1978

The Rule of Metaphor. Multi-Disciplinary Studies of the Creation of Meaning in Language. Translation of La métaphore vive by R. CZERNY with K. McLAUGHLIN and J. COSTELLO and introduced by R. CZERNY. Toronto: University of Toronto Press, 1977; London and Henley: Routledge and Kegan Paul, [1978], 22 x 14, viii-384 p. Paperback print in 1986.

The Philosophy of Paul Ricoeur. An Anthology of His Work (Beacon Paperback 567-Philosophy). Edited and prefaced by Ch. REAGAN and D. STEWART. Boston: Beacon Press, Toronto: Fitzhenry and Whiteside Limited, [1978], 20 x 13,5, vi-262 p.

1979

Main Trends in Philosophy (Main Trends in the Social and Human Sciences, 4). New York-London: Holmes and Meier, [1979], 23 x 15, xvii-469 p.

1980

Essays on Biblical Interpretation. Edited with an introduction by L.S. MUDGE and a reply by P. RICOEUR. Philadelphia: Fortress Press, [1980], 21,5 x 15, ix-182 p.

The Contribution of French Historiography to the Theory of History (The Zaharoff Lecture for 1978-1979). Oxford: Clarendon Press, [New York: Oxford University Press], 1980, 21,5 x 14, 65 p.

1981

Hermeneutics and the Human Sciences. Essays on Language, Action and Interpretation. Edited, translated and introduced by J.B. THOMPSON with a response by P. RICOEUR.

Cambridge - London - New York - New Rochelle - Melbourne - Sydney: Cambridge University Press; Paris: Éditions de la Maison des Sciences de l'Homme, [1981], 23 x 15,5, 314 p. [hardback and paperback].

1984

Time and Narrative. Vol. I. Translation of **Temps et récit I** by K. McLAUGHLIN and D. PELLAUER. Chicago: The University of Chicago Press, [1984], 23,5 x 15,5, xii-274 p.

1985

Time and Narrative. Vol. II. Translation of **Temps et récit II** by K. McLAUGHLIN and D. PELLAUER. Chicago-London: The University of Chicago Press, [1985], 23,5 x 15,5, 208 p.

1986

Lectures on Ideology and Utopia. Edited and introduced by G.H. TAYLOR. New York: Columbia University Press, [1986], 23,5 x 16, xxxvi-353 p.

1988

Time and Narrative. Vol. III. Translation of **Temps et récit III** by K. BLAMEY and D. PELLAUER. Chicago-London: The University of Chicago Press, [1988], 23,5 x 15,5, 355 p.

Articles

1952

"Christianity and the Meaning of History. Progress, Ambiguity, Hope." **The Journal of Religion** 22 (1952), No. 4, October, 242-253.

RICOEUR P. and DOMENACH J.-M., "Mass and Person." **Cross Currents** 2 (1952), Winter, 59-66.

1954

"Sartre's Lucifer and the Lord." **Yale French Studies** 1954-1955, No. 14, Winter, 85-93.

1955

106 " 'Associates' and Neighbor." **Love of Our Neighbor.** Edited by

bibliography A. PLÉ. Springfield (Illinois)-London: Templegate-Blackfriars Publications, 1955, 149-161.

"'Morality Without Sin' or Sin Without Moralism?" **Cross Currents** 5 (1955), No. 4, Fall, 339-352.

"French Protestantism Today." **The Christian Century** 72 (1955), October 26, 1236-1238.

1957

The State and Coercion. The Third John Knox House Lecture, 1957. Geneva: The John Knox House, 1957, 21 x 14,5, 16 p.

"The Relation of Jaspers' Philosophy to Religion." **The Philosophy of Karl Jaspers. A Critical Analysis and Evaluation** (Library of Living Philosophers). Edited by P.A. SCHILPP. New York: Tudor, 1957, 22 x 14,5, 611-642. Reprint: LaSalle (Illinois): Open Court, 1981.

"Faith and Culture." **The Student World**. World's Student Christian Federation (The Greatness and Misery of the Intellectual) 50 (1957), No. 3, 246-251.

1958

"Ye are the Salt of the Earth." **The Ecumenical Review** 10 (1958), No. 3, April, 264-276.

"The Symbol ... Food for Thought." **Philosophy Today** 4 (1960), No. 3/4, Fall, 196-207.

1961

" 'The Image of God' and the Epic of Man." **Cross Currents** 11 (1961), No. 1, Winter, 37-50.

1962

"The Hermeneutics of Symbols and Philosophical Reflection." **International Philosophical Quarterly** 2 (1962), No. 2, 191-218.

1963

"Faith and Action: A Christian Point of View. A Christian must rely on his Jewish memory [expansion of a paper delivered at a conference on "Perspectives on the Good Society," Chicago 1963]." **Criterion** 2 (1963), No. 3, 10-15.

1964

"The Historical Presence of Non-Violence." **Cross Currents** 14 (1964), No. 1, Winter, 15-23.

"The Dimensions of Sexuality. Wonder, Eroticism and Enigma [followed by P. RICOEUR's presentation of the answers to the questionnaire]." **Cross Currents** (Sexuality and the Modern World) 14 (1964), No. 2, Spring, 133-165, 186-208, 229-255.

1966

DUFRENNE M., **The Notion of A Priori** (Northwestern University Studies in Phenomenology and Existential Philosophy). Translation of **La notion a priori** by E. CASEY with a preface of P. RICOEUR. Evanston (Illinois): Northwestern University Press, 1966, 23,5 x 16, ix-xvii.

"The Atheism of Freudian Psychoanalysis." **Concilium** (Church and World) 2 (1966), No. 2, 31-37 [British edition]; **Concilium** (Is God Dead?) 2 (1966), No. 16, 59-72 [American edition].

"Kant and Husserl." **Philosophy Today** 10 (1966), No. 3/4, Fall, 147-168.

"A Conversation...[text of an interview]." **The Bulletin of Philosophy** I (1966), No. 1, January, 1-8.

1967

"Philosophy of Will and Action [talk followed by a discussion with F. KERSTEN *et al.*, at Lexington, (Ky. USA) 1964]." **Phenomenology of Will and Action**. The Second Lexington Conference on Pure and Applied Phenomenology, 1964. Edited by E.W. STRAUS and R.M. GRIFFITH. Pittsburgh: Duquesne University Press, 1967, 22 x 14, 7-33, 34-60.

"Husserl and Wittgenstein on Language." **Phenomenology and Existentialism**. Edited by E.N. LEE and M. MANDELBAUM. Baltimore: The John Hopkins University Press, [1967], 21 x 14, 207-217. Paperback edition in 1969. Reprinted in **Analytic Philosophy and Phenomenology** (American University Publications in Philosophy). Edited by H.A.DURFEE. The Hague: M. Nijhoff, 1976, 24 x 16, 87-95.

"The Unity of the Voluntary and the Involuntary as a Limiting Idea." **Reading in Existential Phenomenology**. Edited by N. LAWRENCE and D. O'CONNOR. Englewood Cliffs (New Jersey): Prentice Hall, [1967], 24 x 17, 390-402. Reprint: New York: Prentice Hall, 1976.

bibliography "New Developments in Phenomenology in France: The Phenomenology of Language." **Social Research** 34 (1967), No. 1, Spring, 1-30.

1968

"The Critique of Subjectivity and Cogito in the Philosophy of Heidegger [text derived from a tape of a paper delivered during the Heidegger Symposium at the De Paul University, Chicago 1966]." **Heidegger and the Quest for Truth**. Edited by M.S. FRINGS. Chicago: Quadrangle Books, 1968, 21,5 x 14,5, 62-75.

"Tasks of the Ecclesial Community in the Modern World." **Theology of Renewal. II. Renewal of Religious Structures**. Edited by L.K. SHOOK [New York]: Herder and Herder, [1968], 21,5 x 15, 242-254.

"Structure-Word-Event." **Philosophy Today** 12 (1968), No. 2/4, Summer, 114-129.

"The Father Image. From Phantasy to Symbol [paper delivered at a seminar on "Hermeneutics and Philosophy of Language," Chicago 1968]. **Criterion**. A Publication of the Divinity School of the University of Chicago 8 (1968-1969), No. 1, Fall-Winter, 1-7.

1969

"The Problem of the Double-Sense as Hermeneutic Problem and as Semantic Problem." **Myths and Symbols**. Studies in Honor of Mircea Eliade. Edited by J.M. KITAGAWA and Ch. H. LONG. Chicago-London: University of Chicago Press, [1969], 22,5 x 14, 63-79.

"Religion, Atheism and Faith [Bampton Lectures in America, delivered at Columbia University, 1966]." **The Religious Significance of Atheism**. Edited by A. MacINTYRE, Ch. ALASDAIR and P. RICOEUR. New York-London: Columbia University Press, 1969, 21 x 14, 58-98. Reprinted in 1986.

"Guilt, Ethics and Religion [paper delivered for the Royal Institute of Philosophy.]" **Talk of God** (Royal Institute of Philosophy Lectures, II. 1967-1968). Edited by G.N.A. VESEY. London-Basingstoke: Macmillan; New York: St. Martin's Press, [1969], 21,5 x 14, 100-117. Reprinted in **Concilium** (Moral Evil Under Challenge) 1970, No. 56, 11-27 [American edition]; **Concilium** (Moral Evil Under Challenge) 6 (1970), No. 6, 11-27 [British edition]. Reprinted in **Conscience: Theological and Psychological Perspectives**. Edited by C.E. NELSON. New York-Paramus-Toronto: Newman, [1973], 22,5 x 15, 11-27.

NABERT J., **Elements of an Ethic** (Northwestern University Studies in Phenomenology and Existential Philosophy). Translation of **Éléments pour une éthique** by W.J. PETREK with a preface by P. RICOEUR. Evanston (Illinois): Northwestern University Press, 1969, 24 x 16, xvii-xxviii.

1970

"Hope and Structure of Philosophical Systems [communication at the American Catholic Association, San Francisco 1970]." **Proceedings of the American Catholic Association** (San Francisco 1970) (Philosophy and Christian Theology). Edited by G.F. McLEAN and F. DOUGHERTY. Washington: The Catholic University of America Press, 1970, 22,5 x 15, 55-69.

"The Problem of the Will and Philosophical Discourse." **Patterns of the Life-World**. Essays in Honor of John Wild (Northwestern Studies in Phenomenology and Existential Philosophy). Edited by J.M. EDIE, F.H. PARKER and C.O. SCHRAG. Evanston (Illinois): Northwestern University Press, 1970, 23,5 x 16, 273-289.

1971

"What is a Text? Explanation and Interpretation." **Mythic-Symbolic Language and Philosophical Anthropology. A Constructive Interpretation of the Thought of Paul Ricoeur** by D.M. RASMUSSEN. The Hague: M. Nijhoff, 1971, 24 x 16, 135-150.

IHDE D., **Hermeneutic Phenomenology. The Philosophy of Paul Ricoeur** (Northwestern University Studies in Phenomenology and Existential Philosophy). Foreword by P. RICOEUR. Evanston: Northwestern University Press, 1971, 23,5 x 15,5, xiii-xvii.

"The Model of the Text: Meaningful Action Considered as a Text." **Social Research** 38 (1971), No. 3, Fall, 529-562. Reprinted in **Social Research** (50th Anniversary, 1934-1984) 51 (1984), Nos. 1 and 2, Spring/Summer, 185-218. Reprinted in **New Literary History** 5 (1973), No. 1, 91-117. Reprinted under the title "Human Sciences and Hermeneutical Method: Meaningful Action Considered as a Text" in **Explorations in Phenomenology** (Selected Studies in Phenomenology and Existential Philosophy, 4). Edited by D. CARR and E.S. CASEY. The Hague: Martinus Nijhoff, 1973, 21 x 14, 13-46.

"From Existentialism to the Philosophy of Language [text of an address before the Divinity School, University of Chicago, 1971]."

bibliography **Criterion** 10 (1971), Spring 14-18. Reprinted in an expanded version under the title "A Philosophical Journey. From Existentialism to the Philosophy of Language" in **Philosophy Today** 17 (1973), No. 2/4, Summer, 88-96.

1973

"Creativity in Language. Word. Polysemy. Metaphor [address delivered at Duquesne University, 1972]." **Philosophy Today** 17 (1973), No. 2/4, Summer, 97-111. Reprinted in **Language and Language Disturbances** (The 5th Lexington Conference on Pure and Applied Phenomenology, 1972). Edited by E.W. STRAUS. Pittsburgh: Duquesne University Press, 1974, 22 x 14,5, 49-71.

"The Task of Hermeneutics [lecture given at Princeton Theological Seminary, 1973]." **Philosophy Today** 17 (1973), No. 2/4, Summer, 112-128. Reprinted in **Exegesis. Problems of Method and Exercises in Reading (Genesis 22 and Luke 15)** (Pittsburgh Theological Monograph Series, 21). Edited by Fr. BOVON and Gr. ROUILLER and translated by D.J. MILLER. Pittsburgh: Pickwick Press, 1978, 21,5 x 14, 265-296 and in **Heidegger and Modern Philosophy. Critical Essays**. Edited by M. MURRAY. New Haven (Conn.): Yale University Press, 1978, 23,5 x 15, 141-160.

"The Hermeneutical Function of Distanciation [lecture given at Princeton Theological Seminary, 1973]." **Philosophy Today** 17 (1973), No. 2/4, Summer, 129-141. Reprinted in **Exegesis. Problems of Method and Exercises in Reading (Genesis 22 and Luke 15)** (Pittsburgh Theological Monograph Series, 21). Edited by Fr. BOVON and Gr. ROUILLER and translated by D.J. MILLER. Pittsburgh: Pickwick Press, 1978, 21,5 x 14, 297-320.

"The Tasks of the Political Educator." **Philosophy Today** 17 (1973), No. 2/4, Summer, 142-152.

"Ethics and Culture. Habermas and Gadamer in Dialogue." **Philosophy Today** 17 (1973), No. 2/4, Summer, 153-165.

"A Critique of B.F. Skinner's **Beyond Freedom and Dignity**." **Philosophy Today** 17 (1973), No. 2/4, Summer, 166-175.

"Metaphor and the Central Problem of Hermeneutics." **Graduate Faculty Philosophy Journal** (New York) 3 (1973-1974), No. 1, 42-58. Reprinted under the title "Metaphor and the Main Problem of Hermeneutics" and, without notes and comment, in **New Literary History** (On Metaphor) 6 (1974-1975), No. 1, 95-110.

"The Critique of Religion." **Union Seminary Quarterly Review** 28 (1973), No. 3, Spring, 203-212.

"The Language of Faith." **Union Seminary Quarterly Review** 28 (1973), No. 3, Spring, 213-224.

1974

"Psychiatry and Moral Values." **American Handbook of Psychiatry. I.** Edited by S. Aricti *et al.* Second edition. New York: Basic Books, 1974, 26 x 18, 976-990.

"Philosophy and Religious Language [lecture delivered under the auspices of the John Nuveen, Chair of Philosophical Theology, University of Chicago]." **The Journal of Religion** 54 (1974), No. 1, 71-85.

"Phenomenology [book review on **Phénoménologie et matérialisme dialectique** by TRAN-DUC-THAO]." **The Southwestern Journal of Philosophy** (Husserl Issue) 5 (1975), No. 3, 149-168.

"Listening to the Parables of Jesus. Text: Matthew 13: 31-32 and 45-46 [sermon]." **Criterion** 13 (1974), No. 3, Spring, 18-22. Reprinted in **Christianity and Crisis** 34 (1975), No. 23, 6 January, 304-308 and I.B.12.

1975

"Phenomenology of Freedom." **Phenomenology and Philosophical Understanding.** Edited with an introduction by E. PIVCEVIC. London-New York-Melbourne: Cambridge University Press, 1975, 21,5 x 13,5, 173-194.

"Phenomenology and Hermeneutics." **Noûs** (Bloomington) 9 (1975), No. 1, 85,102.

"Philosophical Hermeneutics and Theological Hermeneutics." **Studies in Religion. Sciences religieuses** 5 (1975), No. 1, 14-33. Reprinted in **Philosophy of Religion and Theology: 1975 Proceedings.** Reprinted Papers for the Section on Philosophy of Religion and Theology. Compiled by J.W. McCLENDON. The American Academy of Religion, 1975, 23,5 x 15,5, 1-17.

"Biblical Hermeneutics." **Semeia.** An Experimental Journal for Biblical Criticism 1975, No. 4, 27-148. Excerpt (75-88): "The Metaphorical Process [reading]." **Exploring the Philosophy of Religion.** Edited by D.STEWART. Englewood Cliffs (New Jersey): Prentice Hall, [1980], 23 X 15,5 229-238.

1976

GARDET L., GUREVICH. A.J. *et al.*, **Cultures and Time** (At the crossroads of cultures). English translation of **Les cultures et le temps** with an introduction by P. RICOEUR. Paris: The Unesco Press 1976, 24 x 15,5, 13-33.

"Psychoanalysis and the Work of Art [the Edith Weigert Lecture at Washington School of Psychiatry, 1974]." **Psychiatry and the Humanities. I.** Edited by J.H. SMITH. New Haven (Conn.)-London: Yale University Press, 1976, 21,5 x 14,5, 3-33.

"What is Dialectical?" **Freedom and Morality.** The Lindley Lectures delivered at the University of Kansas (University of Kansas Humanistic Studies, 46). Edited with an introduction by J.BRICKE. Lawrence: University of Kansas, 1976, 23 x 15,5, 173-189.

Philosophical Hermeneutics and Theological Hermeneutics: Ideology, Utopia and Faith. Protocol of the Seventeenth Colloquy: 4 November 1975 (Protocol Series of the Colloquies of the Center for Hermeneutical Studies in Hellenistic and Modern Culture, 17) [talk followed by comments and discussions]. Edited by W. WUELLNER. [Berkeley (California)]: The Center for Hermeneutical Studies in Hellenistic and Modern Culture. The Graduate Theological Union and The University of California (Berkeley), [1976], 20 x 16, 1-37, 40-56.

"Ideology and Utopia as Cultural Imagination." **Philosophic Exchange** 2 (1976), No. 2, Summer, 17-28. Reprinted in **Being Human in a Technological Age.** Edited by D.M. BORCHERT and D. STEWART. Athens: Ohio University Press, [1979], 23 x 15, 107-125.

"Philosophical Hermeneutics and Theology." **Theology Digest** 24 (1976), No. 2, 154-161.

"History and Hermeneutics [paper presented at an APA Symposium on Hermeneutics, 1976]." **The Journal of Philosophy** (Symposium: Hermeneutics) 73 (1976), No. 19, 683-695.

"Review Essay. M.Eliade, **Histoire des croyances et des idées religieuses. Vol. I. De l'âge de la pierre aux mystères d'Eleusis.**" **Religious Studies Review** 2 (1976), No. 4, October, 1-4.

1977

STRASSER St., **Phenomenology of Feeling. An Essay on the**

Phenomenon of the Heart (Philosophical Series, 34). Translation and introduction by R.E. WOOD with a foreword by P.RICOEUR. Pittsburgh: Duquesne University Press, 1977, xi-xiv.

AGUESSY H., ASHISH M. *et al.*, **Time and the Philosophies** (At the Crossroads of Cultures). English translation of **Le temps et les philosophies** with an introduction by P. RICOEUR. [Paris]: Unesco, [1977], 24 x 15,5, 13-30.

Husserl. Expositions and Appraisals. Edited with introductions by Fr. A. ELLISTON and P. McCORMICK and with a foreword by P. RICOEUR. Notre Dame (Ind.)-London: University of Notre Dame Press, [1977], 25 x 17,5, ix-xi.

Hermeneutic of the Idea of Revelation. Protocol of the Twenty-Seventh Colloquy: 13 February 1977 (Protocol Series of the Colloquies of the Center for Hermeneutical Studies in Hellenistic and Modern Culture, 27) [talk followed by comments and discussions]. Edited by W. WUELLNER. [Berkeley (California)]: The Center for Hermeneutical Studies in Hellenistic and Modern Culture. The Graduate Theological Union and the University of California (Berkeley), [1977], 20 x 15, 5, 1-23, 25-36.

"Phenomenology and the Social Sciences." **The Annals of Phenomenological Sociology** 2 (1977), 145-159.

"The Question of Proof in Freud's Psychoanalytic Writings." **Journal of the American Psychoanalytic Association** 25 (1977), No. 4, 835-871.

"Toward a Hermeneutic of the Idea of Revelation." **Harvard Theological Review** 70 (1977), No. 1-2, January-April, 1-37.

"Patocka. Philosopher and Resister." **Telos** 1977, No. 31, Spring, 152-155.

"Schleiermacher's Hermeneutics." **The Monist** (Philosophy and Religion in the 19th Century) 60 (1977), No. 2, April, 181-197.

"Writing as Problem for Literary Criticism and Philosophical Hermeneutics." **Philosophic Exchange** 2 (1977), No. 3, Summer, 3-15.

"Construing and Construction. Book Review: E.D. HIRSCH, Jr., **The Aims of Interpretation.**" The Times Literary Supplement 197 (1977), No. 3911, February 25, 216.

1978

114   "4. Philosophy." **Main Trends of Research in the Social and**

bibliography   **Human Sciences. Part two/Volume two: Legal Science/
Philosophy**. Under the editorship of J. HAVET. The Hague-
Paris-New York: Mouton-Unesco, 1978, 25 x 17, 1071-1567.

"Philosophical Hermeneutics and Biblical Hermeneutics."
**Exegesis. Problems of Method and Exercises in Reading
(Genesis 22 and Luke 15)** (Pittsburgh Theological Monograph
Series, 21). Edited by Fr. BOVON and Gr. ROUILLER and
translated D.J. MILLER. Pittsburgh: Pickwick Press, 1978, 21,5
x 14, 321-339.

"History and Hermeneutics [with a comment by Ch.TAYLOR]."
Philosophy of History and Action. Papers of the First
Jerusalem Philosophical Encounter, 1974 (Philosophical Studies
Series in Philosophy, 11). Edited by Y. YOVEL. Dordrecht-
Boston-London-Jerusalem: D. Reidel Publishing Company - The
Magnes Press (Hebrew University), [1978], 22,5 x 16, 3-25.

"Panel Discussion. Is a Philosophy of History Possible? [with I.
BERLIN, St. HAMPSHIRE, M. BLACK *et al.*]." **Philosophy of
History and Action**. Papers of the First Jerusalem Philosophical
Encounter, 1974 (Philosophical Studies Series in Philosophy,
11). Edited by Y. YOVEL. Dordrecht-Boston-London-Jerusalem:
D. Reidel Publishing Company - The Magnes Press (Hebrew
University), [198], 22,5 x 16, 219-240.

"Can There Be a Scientific Concept of Ideology?"
Phenomenology and the Social Sciences: A Dialogue. Edited
by J. BIEN. The Hague-Boston-London: M. Nijhoff, 1978, 24 x 16,
44-59.

"Imagination in Discourse and in Action." **The Human Being in
Action. The Irreducible Element in Man. Part II. Investigation
at the Intersection of Philosophy and Psychiatry (Analecta
Husserliana**, 7). Edited by A.-T. TYMIENIECKA. Dordrecht-
Boston-London: D. Reidel Publishing Company, 1978, 23 x 15,5,
3-22.

"Image and Language in Psychoanalysis." **Psychoanalysis and
Language** (Psychiatry and the Humanities, 3). Edited by J.H.
SMITH. New Haven-London: Yale University Press, 1978, 21,5 x
15, 293-324.

"The Narrative Function." **Semeia** 1978, No. 13, 177-202.

"The Problem of the Foundation of Moral Philosophy."
Philosophy Today 22 (1978), No. 3-4, Fall, 175-192.

115   "Response to Karl Rahner's Lecture: On the Incomprehensibility
of God." **Celebrating the Medieval Heritage. A Colloquy on the**

Thought of Aquinas and Bonaventure (Supplement to The Journal of Religion 58) (1978). Edited by D. TRACY, 23 X 15, S 126-S 131.

RICOEUR P. *et al.*, "Conference on Religious Studies and the Humanities: Theories of Interpretation. November 17-19, 1977. First Session: Paul Ricoeur [paper of P. RICOEUR reproduced by B.E. LAWRENCE]." Criterion 17 (1978), No. 2, Summer, 20-23, 23-29.

"The Metaphorical Process as Cognition, Imagination and Feeling." Critical Inquiry (On Metaphor) 5 (1978), No. 1, Fall, 143-159. Reprinted in On Metaphor. Edited by Sh. SACKS. [Chicago-London]: The University of Chicago Press, [1979], 23 x 15, 141-157. Paperback edition in 1980. Reprinted in Philosophical Perspectives on Metaphor. Edited by M. JOHNSON. Minneapolis: University of Minnesota Press, [1981], 23,5 x 16, 228-247.

TOULMIN St., "Psychoanalysis, Physics and the Mind-Body Problem, with discussion by P. RICOEUR." The Annual of Psychoanalysis 6 (1978), November, 315-342.

"That Fiction 'Remakes' Reality." The Journal of the Blaisdell Institute 12 (1978), No. 1, Winter, 44-62.

"My Relation to the History of Philosophy." The Iliff Review (Paul Ricoeur's Philosophy) 35 (1978), No. 3, Fall, 5-12.

1979

Studies in the Philosophy of Paul Ricoeur. Edited by Ch. E. REAGAN with a preface by P. RICOEUR. Athens (Ohio): Ohio University Press, [1979], 23,5 x 16, xi-xxi.

LACOCQUE A., The Book of Daniel. Translation of Le livre de Daniel by D. PELLAUER with a foreword by P. RICOEUR. London-Atlanta: S.P.C.K.-J. Knox Press, 24 x 16, [1979], xvii-xxvi.

"Hegel and Husserl on Intersubjectivity." Reason, Action and Experience. Essays in Honor of Raymond Klibansky. Edited by H. KOHLENBERGER. Hamburg: Felix Meiner Verlag, [1979], 23,5 x 16, 13-29.

"Epilogue. The 'Sacred' Text and the Community." The Critical Study of Sacred Texts (Berkeley Religious Studies Series). Edited by W.D. O'FLAHERTY. Berkeley: [Graduate Theological Union], 1979, 22,5 x 16, 271-276.

bibliography RICOEUR P., HABERMAS J. *et al.*, "Discussion [on the paper: J. HABERMAS, "Aspects of the Rationality of Action"]." **Rationality Today. La rationalité aujourd'hui** (Philosophica, 13). Edited by Th. F. GERAETS. Ottawa: The University of Ottawa Press - Éditions de l'Université d'Ottawa, 1979, 23 x 15, 205-212.

"Naming God." **Union Seminary Quarterly Review** 34 (1979), No. 4, Summer, 215-228.

"The Hermeneutics of Testimony." **Anglican Theological Review** 61 (1979), No.4, 435-461.

"The Human Experience of Time and Narrative." **Research in Phenomenology** (Studies in Phenomenology and the Human Sciences. Papers presented at the Human Sciences at Duquesne University, 1978) 9 (1979), 17-34.

"The Function of Fiction in Shaping Reality." **Man and World** 12 (1979), No. 2, 123-141.

"A Response [to the papers of A. LACOCQUE, D. CROSSAN and L.S. MUDGE]." **Biblical Research** (Symposium: Paul Ricoeur and Biblical Hermeneutics) 24-25 (1979-1980), 70-80.

"The Logic of Jesus, the Logic of God [sermon delivered in Rockefeller Chapel at the University of Chicago]." **Criterion** 18 (1979), No. 2, Summer, 4-6. Reprinted in **Anglican Theological Review** 62 (1980), No. 1, January, 37-41.

1980

"Narrative Time." **Critical Inquiry** (On Narrative) 7 (1980), No. 1, Autumn, 169-190. Reprinted in **On Narrative**. Edited by W.J.T. MITCHELL. Chicago-London: The University of Chicago Press, [1981], 23 x 15,5, 165-186.

"Ways of Worldmaking, by Nelson Goodman [critical discussion]." **Philosophy and Literature** 4 (1980), No. 1, Spring, 107-120.

1981

MADISON G. Br., **The Phenomenology of Merleau-Ponty. A Search for the Limits of Consciousness**. Foreword by P. RICOEUR. Athens (Ohio): University Press, [1981], 23,5 x 16, xiii-xix.

"Sartre and Ryle on the Imagination." **The Philosophy of Jean-Paul Sartre** (The Library of Living Philosophers, 26). Edited by

P.A. SCHLIPP. La Salle (Illinois): Open Court, [1981], 23,5 x 16, 167-178.

"The Bible and the Imagination." **The Bible as a Document of the University** (Polibridge Books, 3). Edited by H.D. BETZ with a foreword by M.E. MARTY. [Chico (California)]: Scholar Press, [1981], 22,5 x 14,5, 49-75.

"Two Encounters with Kierkegaard: Kierkegaard and Evil. Doing Philosophy after Kierkegaard." **Kierkegaard's Truth: The Discourse of the Self** (Psychiatry and Humanities, 5). Edited by J.H. SMITH. New Haven-London: Yale University Press, [1981], 22 x 15, 313-342.

"Mimesis and Representation." **Annals of Scholarship**. Metastudies of the Humanities and Social Sciences 2 (1981), No. 3, 15-32.

"The 'Kingdom' in the Parables of Jesus." **Anglican Theological Review** 63 (1981), No. 2, April, 165-169.

"Phenomenology and Theory of Literature. An Interview with Paul Ricoeur [by E. NAKJAVANI]." **MLN-Modern Language Notes** (Comparative Literature) 96 (1981), No. 5, December, 1084-1090.

1982

GADAMER H.-G. and RICOEUR P., "The Conflict of Interpretations [introductory texts by both philosophers followed by a discussion between them. Partial transcription from the recording of a symposium]." **Phenomenology: Dialogues and Bridges** (Selected studies in Phenomenology and Existential Philosophy, 8). Edited by R. BRUZINA and Br. WILSHIRE. Albany: State University of New York Press, [1982], 23,5 x 15,5, 299-320 [cloth and paper].

"The Status of *Vorstellung* in Hegel's Philosophy of Religion." **Meaning, Truth and God** (Boston University Studies in Philosophy and Religion, 3). Edited by L.S. ROUNER. Notre Dame-London: University of Notre Dame Press, [1982], 24 x 16, 70-88.

"Poetry and Possibility: An Interview with Paul Ricoeur Conducted by Philip Ried." **The Manhattan Review** 2 (1982), No. 2, 6-21.

1983

118 "On Interpretation." **Philosophy in France Today**. Edited by A.

bibliography   MONTEFIORE. Cambridge-London-New York-New Rochelle-Melbourne-Sydney: Cambridge University Press, [1983], 22 x 14,5, 175-197 [Hard cover and paperback edition]. Reprinted in **After Philosophy. End or Transformation?** Edited by K. BAYNES *et al.* Cambridge (Massachusetts)-London: The MIT Press, [1987], 23,5 x 15, 357-380.

" 'Anatomy of Criticism' or the Order of Paradigms [on N. FRYE, **Anatomy of Criticism**]." **Centre and Labyrinth**. Essays in Honour of Northrop Frye. Edited by E. COOK, Ch. HOSEK *et al.* Toronto-Buffalo-London: University of Toronto Press, [1983], 23,5 x 16, 1-13.

"Can Fictional Narratives Be True (Inaugural Essay)." **The Phenomenology of Man and of the Human Condition. Individualisation of Nature and of the Human Being. I.** Plotting the Territory for Interdisciplinary Communication (**Analecta Husserliana.** The Yearbook of Phenomenological Research, XIV). Edited by A.-T. TYMIENIECKA. Dordrecht-Boston-London: D. Reidel, [1983], 23 x 16, 3-19.

"Narrative and Hermeneutics." **Essays on Aesthetics**. Perspectives on the Work of Monroe C. Beardsley. Edited by J. FISHER. Philadelphia: Temple University Press, [1983], 23,5 x 16, 149-160.

"Action, Story and History: On Re-reading **The Human Condition** [by H. ARENDT]." **Salmagundi**. A Quarterly of the Humanities and Social Sciences (On Hannah Arendt) 1983, No. 60, Spring-Summer, 60-72.

"Jan Patocka: A Philosopher of Resistance." **The Crane Bag**. Journal of Irish Studies 7 (1983), No. 1, 116-118.

1984

The Reality of the Historical Past (The Aquinas Lecture, 1984, No. 48). Under the Auspices of the Wisconsin-Alpha Chapter of Sigma Tau. Milwaukee: Marquette University Press, 1984, 18,5 x 11,5, 51 p.

"Gabriel Marcel and Phenomenology. Reply [of G. MARCEL] to Paul Ricoeur." **The Philosophy of Gabriel Marcel** (The Library of Living Philosophers, 17). Edited by P.A. SCHELPP and C. HAHN. La Salle (Illinois): Open Court, [1984], 23,5 x 16,5, 471-498.

"Ideology and ideology critique." **Phenomenology and Marxism** (International Library of Phenomenology and Moral Sciences).

vansina

Edited by B. WALDENFELS, J. BROEKMAN and A. PAZANIN
and translated by S.Cl. EVANS. London: Routledge and Kegan
Paul, [1984], 22,5 x 14, 134-164.

KEARNEY R., "[Dialogues with] Paul Ricoeur. Prefatory Note. I:
The Creativity of Language. II: Myth as the Bearer of Possible
Worlds." **Dialogues with Contemporary Continental thinkers.
The Phenomenological Heritage. Paul Ricoeur. Emmanuel
Levinas. Herbert Marcuse. Stanislas Breton. Jacques
Derrida**. [Manchester]: Manchester University Press, [1984],
22,3 x 14,3, 15-46. A shortened version of the second dialogue
appeared in **The Crane Bag**. Journal of Irish Studies 2 (1978),
No. 1-2, 260-266. Paperback reprint in 1986.

"From Proclamation to Narrativity [a study in the light of
Rediscovering the Teaching of Jesus by N. PERRIN]." **The
Journal of Religion** 64 (1984), No. 4, October, 501-612.

"Toward a 'Post-Critical Rhetoric'? [response of P. RICOEUR on
the double issue of **Pretext** on "Ricoeur and Rhetoric"]." **Pretext**
5 (1984), Spring, No. 1, 9-16.

1985

"The History of Religions and the Phenomenology of Time
Consciousness." **The History of Religions. Retrospect and
Prospect**. Edited by J.M. KIAGAWA with an afterward by G.D.
ALLES and the editor. New York-London: Macmillan, [1985], 24
x 16, 13-30.

"The Text as Dynamic Identity." **Identity of the Literary Text**.
Edited by M.J. VALDÉS and O. MILKO. Toronto-Buffalo-London:
University of Toronto Press, [1985], 22,8 x 15, 175-186.

"Evil, a Challenge to Philosophy and Theology [paper presented
as a Plenary Address to the 75th Anniversary Annual Meeting of
the American Academy of Religion, 1984]." **Journal of the
American Academy of Religion**, 53 (1985), No. 4, December,
635-638. Reprinted in **Gottes Zukunft-Zukunft der Welt**.
Festschrift für Jürgen Moltmann zum 60. Geburtstag. Edited by H.
DEUSER et al. [Munich]: Kaiser Verlag, [1986], 23,3 x 15,5, 345-
361.

"Irrationality and the Plurality of the Philosophical Systems
(Summary. Résumé. Zusammentassing)." **Dialectica** 39 (1985),
No. 4, 297-319.

120 "The Power Speech: Science and Poetry." **Philosophy Today** 29
(1985), No. 1/4, Spring, 59-70.

bibliography

"History as Narrative and Practice. Peter Kemp talks to Paul Ricoeur in Copenhagen." **Philosophy Today** 29 (1985), No. 3/4, Fall, 213-222.

"Narrated Time [first draft of the conclusions on time in the forthcoming Volume III of **Time and Narrative**]." **Philosophy Today** 29 (1985), No. 4/4, Winter, 259-272.

1986

Philosophical Foundations of Human Rights. Edited and introduced by P. RICOEUR. Paris: Unesco, 1986, 9-29.

"Life: A Story in Search of a Narrator." **Facts and Values. Philosophical Reflections from Western and Non-Western Perspectives** (Martinus Nijhoff Philosophy Library, 19). Edited by M.C. DOESER and N. KRAAJ. Dordrecht-Boston-Lancaster: Nijhoff, 1986, 24,5 x 16,5, 121-132.

DAUENHAUER B.P., **The Politics of Hope** (Criterical Social Thought). Foreword by P. RICOEUR. New York-London: Routledge and Kegan Paul, [1986], 22 x 14, ix-xvi.

1987

The Greatness and Fragility of Political Language. The Forty-Second John Findley Green Foundation Lecture [delivered at Westminster College, Fulton (Missouri), 1987]. [Fulton (Missouri), 1987], 21,5 x 14, 11 p. A slightly different version is published under the title "The Fragility of Political Language" in **Philosophy Today** 31 (1987), No. 1/4, Spring, 35-53.

BARASH J.A., **Martin Heidegger and the Problem of Historical Meaning (Phænomenologica,**102). Preface by P. RICOEUR. Dordrecht-Boston-Lancaster: M. Nijhoff, 1987, 24,5 x 16,5, IX-XVIII.

"Evil." **The Encyclopedia of Religion. Vol. 5.** Editor in chief M. ELIADE. New York-London: Macmillan, [1987], 28,5 x 22,5, 199-208.

"Myth and History." **The Encyclopedia of Religion. Vol. 10.** Editor in chief M. ELIADE. New York-London, [1987], 28,5 x 22,5 273-282.

"The Teleological and Deontological Structure of Action: Aristotle and/or Kant?" **Contemporary French Philosophy** (Royal Institute of Philosophy Lecture Series, 21). Edited by A. PHILLIPS GRIFFITHS. Cambridge - New York - New Rochelle - Melbourne-Sydney: Cambridge University Press, [1987], 23 x 16, 99-111.

121